THROUGH THE LENS

THE PANDEMIC AND BLACK LIVES MATTER

PRAISE FOR *CONVERSATIONS ON CONFLICT PHOTOGRAPHY* BY LAUREN WALSH

"[H]ighbrow, brilliant, striking, [and] thoughtful." – *New York Magazine*

"This book offers an extraordinary window into the world of conflict photographers. Traditionally, conflict photographers have been hailed for their bravery on the frontlines. Over and over, I've seen that their role is far broader and far more important. They are groundbreaking journalists whose images document war crimes, violence, and human rights abuses and help bring perpetrators to justice."
– David Rohde, Pulitzer Prize winner, *The New Yorker*

"Photographers have the most dangerous job in journalism because they have to go where the action is. Their images have deepened understanding and changed perceptions. But the cost has been high…*Conversations on Conflict Photography* allows the photojournalists who bore witness to step out from behind the lens and tell their own stories. We owe it to them to stop and listen."
– Joel Simon, Executive Director of the Committee to Protect Journalists

"*Conversations on Conflict Photography* will no doubt be a go-to book for anyone studying visual journalism. It humanizes what it means to negotiate the business of photographing and reporting on crisis issues by providing a diverse array of viewpoints by many seasoned professionals."
– Karen Marshall, Chair of the Documentary Practice and Visual Journalism Program, International Center of Photography

"In this important and timely book, Walsh guides the reader into the lives and thoughts of key photographers and industry professionals who do so much to shape our understanding of international affairs. Her concise summary of the key questions and challenges of conflict reporting is expanded on by her extensive series of interviews that capture the authoritative and authentic voices of those who act as the conduit through which we experience the lives of others caught up in conflict."
– Paul Lowe, Professor of Documentary Photography, University of the Arts London

"In this era of disinformation, circulation of rumors, and threats to journalism, with a public that exhibits apathy and skepticism related to the infobesity, the work of Lauren Walsh is crucial to defending the ideals of photography." – Christophe Deloire, Secretary General and Executive Director, Reporters Sans Frontières / Reporters Without Borders

"The bravest people in the world, and the foolhardy, are conflict photographers. My basic rule for covering wars is never to accept a ride from a photographer or video journalist: When they hear gunfire, they rush toward it. This book is a collection of interviews with photographers about the work they do, why they do it and the ethical issues they confront—including many of their most searing images. We all owe these photographers a debt for their courage and for forcing us to face the reality and brutality of war." – Nicholas Kristof, Pulitzer Prize winner, *New York Times*

"*Conversations on Conflict Photography* is about the ethics of our work. It's about imposition and intent. It's about apathy. It's about putting your life at risk to tell a story no one may ever see. It's about the moral imperative of telling the news." – *LensCulture*

"Navigating complex issues with nuance and grace, and complemented by the visceral power of 110 photos, this is a profound and insightful collection that will encourage readers to reflect deeply on the questions it raises." – *LSE*

"Cultural critic, writer and professor Lauren Walsh intrepidly enters the complex terrain of media literacy to deliver a twenty-first century paradigm of photojournalism." – *ZEKE*, The Magazine of Global Documentary

ALSO BY LAUREN WALSH

Conversations on Conflict Photography

Shadow of Memory
with Ron Haviv

The Millennium Villages Project
Co-edited with Ron Haviv and Gary Knight

Macondo: Memories of the Colombian Conflict
Editor

The Future of Text and Image:
Collected Essays on Literary and Visual Conjunctures
Co-edited with Ofra Amihay

THROUGH THE LENS

THE PANDEMIC AND BLACK LIVES MATTER

LAUREN WALSH

First published 2022
by Routledge
4 Park Square, Milton Park, Abingdon, Oxon OX14 4RN

and by Routledge
605 Third Avenue, New York, NY 10158

Routledge is an imprint of the Taylor & Francis Group, an informa business

British Library Cataloguing-in-Publication Data
A catalogue record for this book is available from the British Library

Library of Congress Cataloging-in-Publication Data
Names: Walsh, Lauren, interviewer.
Title: Through the Lens : The Pandemic and Black Lives Matter / Lauren Walsh.
Description: Abingdon, Oxon ; New York, NY : Routledge, 2022. | Includes bibliographical references and index.
Identifiers: LCCN 2021047810 (print) | LCCN 2021047811 (ebook) | ISBN 9781032186153 (paperback) | ISBN 9781032186146 (hardback) | ISBN 9781003255383 (ebook)
Subjects: LCSH: Photojournalists—Interviews. | Photojournalists—United States—Interviews. | Editors—United States—Interviews. | COVID-19 Pandemic, 2020- | Black Lives Matter movement.
Classification: LCC TR820 .W3525 2022 (print) | LCC TR820 (ebook) | DDC 777.0973—dc23/eng/20211005
LC record available at https://lccn.loc.gov/2021047810
LC ebook record available at https://lccn.loc.gov/2021047811

ISBN: 978-1-032-18614-6 (hbk)
ISBN: 978-1-032-18615-3 (pbk)
ISBN: 978-1-003-25538-3 (ebk)

DOI: 10.4324/9781003255383

Publisher's Note
This book has been prepared from camera-ready copy provided by Lauren Walsh (author) and Stephanie Leone (book designer).

Typeset in Helvetica Neue by Stephanie Leone.

To Isabelle and Annaliese,
In hopes that our visions for a future free from injustice and suffering may come true.

CONTENTS

1 INTRODUCTION

///

On January 6, 2021, the world watched as the United States Capitol Building was breached by insurrectionists. The chaos of the day resulted in the deaths of five people along with extensive damage to the building itself. Many of the rioters self-documented with cell phones, but the general public, in both the US and abroad, watched these extraordinary events unfold because the media was there—and particularly, because visual journalists were there, documenting with cameras.

Figure 1.1 / Rioters threaten and chase officer Eugene Goodman inside the Capitol, January 6, 2021.

© Ashley Gilbertson/VII

That day was labeled a "siege" and comparisons were made to the American Civil War.[1] In fact, we learned in the wake of January 6, that the term "civil war" had been part of the conversation among individuals who helped organize the event.[2] The bellicose rhetoric even proliferated in the aftermath. It was "the worst attack"; it was "the greatest assault"; it was an "invasion."[3]

Figure 1.2 / A rioter smashes a window of the Capitol Building, January 6, 2021.

© Christopher Lee for *Time*

Figure 1.3 / Rioters inside an office in the Capitol Building, January 6, 2021.

© Ron Haviv/VII

But while this early 2021 date readily invited discussion of a home-grown war, the reality is that the *preceding* year was, arguably, one of the most conflicted in American history.

Wars take lives. Wars tear at the social fabric. Yet the US witnessed both of these outcomes, and more, in 2020 without *any* declarations of war. January 6 serves as an exemplary case for observing the crucial journalistic impact of imagery, as well as the vast reach of it, distilled into one single day. But it was 2020 as a whole, a period of groundbreaking social and political upheaval, in combination with a colossal epidemiological crisis, that rescripted our lives and redefined the working conditions of photojournalists.

So while there is much to be said about the spectacle nature of January 6 and attendant issues for press photographers, for this discussion, I am treating it as a culmination—a highly visual coda, of sorts, to a year that witnessed egregious political polarization, enormous racial reckoning, and the politicization of a pandemic, all of which played out in the news. And the dissemination of news, of course, is today unthinkable without images. To that end, the purpose of *Through the Lens: The Pandemic and Black Lives Matter* is to take a deeper look at the months prior to January 6, examining the multilayered conflicts that profoundly marked 2020, and especially to consider the intricacies of documenting and distributing the news with a camera.

2020, A GLOBAL GAME-CHANGER

As we well know, amidst all else that unfolded that year, 2020 can be defined by two historic upheavals, both of which move the conversation from the United States onto the global stage: the Covid-19 pandemic and the explosion of the Black Lives Matter (BLM) movement.

Covid-19 is a once-in-a-century occurrence that, as of this writing, has taken nearly four million lives around the world. The 2020 Black Lives Matter protests were the largest demonstrations in United States history and reverberated internationally.[4] The former is the work of an "invisible" viral enemy while the latter directly relies on its visibility for political power. Both situations have presented unique challenges for photojournalism and public engagement. Significantly, both have forced photographers into a terrain defined by new ethical, technological, and safety (emotional as well as physical) concerns.

This collection of interviews, with photojournalists and photo editors, addresses those new challenges from the firsthand perspectives of those who covered 2020's biggest stories. These glimpses into the difficulties, dangers, and shifting expectations during this extraordinary year offer insight into a wider field of journalistic experience. The emphasis here is more heavily on American practitioners, particularly in grappling with the coverage of Black Lives Matter, as it was this imagery that influenced the global BLM response. However, the inclusion of international voices—one from Wuhan, the originating point of the virus, and the other from Peru, which has had the highest per capita Covid mortality rate in the world—both deepens the conversation and shows how, at times, the experience of documenting crisis or death can be similar, no matter where one is in the world.[5]

Through the Lens exists as a special companion edition to my book *Conversations on Conflict Photography*, which explores the myriad nuances of photojournalistic coverage of war and humanitarian crisis. This volume also operates as a stand-alone compilation of interviews, documenting how the critical upheavals of 2020 massively impacted the realm of photojournalism.

THE LANDSCAPE

On May 25, 2020, George Floyd, a Black American man, was murdered by then Minneapolis police officer Derek Chauvin, who pinned Floyd to the ground and pressed his knee into his victim's neck until he no longer drew breath.[6] Floyd, of course, was not the first Black American killed by a white officer and as 2020 unfolded, we learned he would also not be the last. But this killing was a turning point. It sparked an unprecedented reaction, likely influenced by a number of factors, including the existence of a nine-and-a-half minute video documenting the last moments of Floyd's life, and by the pandemic itself, which had, for the preceding months, forced many in the US to live an isolated existence. The horrifying video and the need to feel engaged with others, alongside the sentiment that public systems were failing many Americans in the midst of the epidemic, drove record numbers of people to take to the streets and demand justice.[7]

What pushed these events beyond US borders was, in part, the media itself. The Black Lives Matter protests received more media attention than any other US protests in the last half century.[8] From there, we witnessed what the BBC called a "global phenomenon"—or, as the *New York Times* put it, it "began with a video" and "shook the world."[9] This wave of anger and demonstration—which rose and crashed down in every single continent save Antarctica—would not have occurred without the imagery produced in the United States, depicting the outpouring of emotion that swelled in reaction to Floyd's death.[10]

In Belgium, for instance, activists didn't just react to the visuals from America but demanded the removal of their country's own visible legacies of colonial abuse:

> For nearly a century, a statue of Belgian King Léopold II has stood sentinel in front of the royal palace in the center of Brussels, cast in metal from the mines of a nation that was once his personal property: the Belgian Congo. Now, thousands of protesters are demanding it be torn down, spurred by the Black Lives Matter protests in the United States.[11]

In Rio de Janeiro, hundreds gathered in May 2020 to protest the deaths of Black and favela youth at the hands of Brazilian police.[12] Meanwhile, African media, in Kenya, South Africa, and beyond, "closely followed the Black Lives Matter protests in the United States, almost always in solidarity with the protesters." In turn, reports the Council on Foreign Relations, there were protests across the continent, condemning local police brutality.[13] And the list of global responses goes on and on.

The backdrop for these historic protests—which stand atop a history of institutionalized racism in the United States and signify related systematized injustices around the globe—was the Covid-19 pandemic. It began in Wuhan, China in late 2019, and during the ensuing months, there was little epidemiological agreement on what exactly this virus did to the body and how exactly it was transmitted. Epicenters moved around the globe, from Wuhan to Italy to New York and elsewhere. The WHO [World Health Organization] and the CDC [the US Centers for Disease Control and Prevention] didn't fully understand what was happening and this led, at times, to panic and missteps.[14] All the while, media outlets convulsed the public with minute-to-minute coverage and anxious questions: Can I get sick from my groceries? Is six feet far enough apart? Will my dog catch it, or give it to me? Twenty-year-olds are safe, right?

Although the public hungered for news, in reality, the pandemic provided a golden opportunity for the suppression of the free movement of information. The year witnessed "a dramatic deterioration" in access to information globally, according to Reporters Without Borders: "The coronavirus pandemic has been used as grounds to block journalists' access to information sources and reporting in the field."[15] Beyond citing the virus as a reason—albeit an illegitimate one—to restrict journalists' activities, many governments, globally, didn't want accurate reporting on the virus itself, as such reporting would reveal massive infrastructural failures. For instance, Peru, which witnessed one of the highest excess death rates in the world, underreported its death tolls and public healthcare issues.[16] Associated Press photographer Rodrigo Abd [Chapter 5], who is based there, addresses this in his interview: "It's a terrible situation for the local news" because despite the reality of what's happening on the ground, he explains, regional media face steep challenges and can fall prey to retribution if they report in ways that raise flags.[17] At the same time, Peru has seen one of the highest Covid-19 death rates among journalists, revealing just how dangerous such coverage is.[18] The truth-telling documentarian risks ending up on the wrong side of both the authorities and the virus itself.

As regards press freedom, China has long been censured by Western pro-democracy organizations for its policies of suppression and censorship.[19] Local coverage of the pandemic was no exception. Reuters photographer Aly Song [Chapter 6], who is based in Shanghai and documented Covid-19's impact in Wuhan in early 2020, describes in his interview a moment when "we fought to keep this imagery" from inside a Covid treatment facility. But it was imagery that local politicians hadn't authorized, and so Song was forced to delete his work.

Beyond Peru's under-reporting and China's repressive actions, 2020 demonstrated that censorship exists all around the world. According to Reporters Without Borders, 73% of the countries the organization analyzed "are classified as having 'very bad,' 'bad' or 'problematic' environments for press freedom."[20] These are daunting numbers for a public that hopes to be informed and for the journalists themselves who take personal risks to bring information to the public.

ETHICAL ISSUES AND JOURNALISTIC OBSTACLES

These interviews about 2020's momentous coverage are modeled after interviews I conducted for my book, *Conversations on Conflict Photography*. They give voice to a breadth of key practitioners and emphasize the ethical and security challenges they face in creating and disseminating photographs, as well as the moral conundrums their work forces us, the viewing audience, to contend with. The following subsections highlight some of those challenges, providing context for the thoughts and experiences of the interviewees in *Through the Lens.*

/ Privacy Versus Visibility

How should the photojournalist balance the privacy of an individual subject against the public's need to see and know? This dilemma played out, in differing ways, in the coverage of both the pandemic and Black Lives Matter.

With Covid-19, photographers wanting to convey the extent of the disease felt hampered at times by a lack of hospital access. Even with access, as both photo editors interviewed here describe, there can be hospital restrictions, some of which exist to protect patients' privacy; those restrictions, in turn, made it harder to document faces and individual stories. Some critics have pointed out that the Trump administration, while loosening certain hospital privacy restrictions, held fast on the media constraints.[21] Yet if the public had seen more extreme physical suffering, even death, early on in the pandemic in American media, would we have taken this virus more seriously? (As a reminder, in February 2020, President Trump referred to the virus as the Democrats' "new hoax." His base believed him.)[22] Indeed, Sarah Elizabeth Lewis, an art historian at Harvard, questioned why US news was not more consistently showing the public the very tough images of severe illness from Covid. "Statistics alone, however clear, are not historically how we have communicated calamity on this scale," she writes. "There is an inverse relationship between high numbers and comprehension: It is much harder to picture tragedy of the kind we are now witnessing than it is to visualize one person in pain, or an image that connects with a familiar aspect of the human condition, what psychologists have termed the 'identifiable victim effect.'"[23] In short, putting a human face to the carnage has a greater impact on the viewer.

But the claim that we should be seeing other people's extreme misery or their dying moments is incredibly complicated. Photographers in this collection, some of whom have spent time working abroad and covering faraway suffering, now faced a crisis at home. Should one document differently—more circumspectly, or with more of an emphasis on giving dignity to the sufferer—when photographing in your own backyard? It is known that Western viewers "look differently" at such imagery. They tend to be far more critical of photography that captures graphic suffering when the victim is local or looks like them. There is, as a sympathetic critic might explain it, a more profound experience of "that could be me." Others would simply label it hypocrisy, ethnocentrism, or racism. Viewers, however, can feel their objections are well motivated, that they're sympathizing with victims and their families, and thus wanting to safeguard them from prying eyes. In the end, this jumble of emotions elicits, at times, angry reactions directed at the photographer for not protecting a victim's identity or for creating lurid imagery.[24]

Getty Images photographer Spencer Platt [Chapter 4], who didn't gain early access to a hospital, talks about taking photos in public and what this means for the personal privacy of the subject. Speaking about images of patients on stretchers, he observes, "They are not easy pictures to look at, but the threat this pandemic has posed outweighs an approach full of niceties." At the same time, he acknowledges that covering conflict at home has forced him to think more carefully about tropes of suffering. Peru-based photographer Abd is also sensitive to the rights of photographed subjects, for instance, obtaining consent if photographing in private spaces like someone's home. He is nevertheless adamant that intimate images of death must be part of the coverage: "[Y]ou need to show exactly what is going on. It's the only way to document the truth of the story."

/ Evolving Notions of Photojournalism

The privacy versus visibility debate plays out differently in BLM coverage. While critics argued for showing individual Covid victims and their private suffering, the Black Lives Matter protests in the US, by contrast, witnessed a new turn in the conversation, as some advocated that the photographic documentation should not isolate individual faces amid this collective display of outrage. Those who covered the protests found themselves caught up in evolving notions of what is acceptable or responsible documentary practice in public spaces. This was largely driven by updates in surveillance and concerns that new technologies can read identities in photographs, potentially putting activists at risk of retaliation by police.[25] Photojournalists faced demands that they either not photograph, blur faces, or get express consent from individuals they have photographed.

Nina Berman [Chapter 2], a photographer based in New York, reacts to that last point:

> Prior to this 2020 conversation, there was a strong consensus that with protests, and really any activities in public, journalists didn't need to ask consent of people they were photographing because there is no expectation of privacy when someone is out on the street at a political event. And to ask consent is antithetical to what journalists are supposed to do, which is to witness and document. Now this view is being called into question, and I and others are reflecting on it, because of the use of facial recognition technology.

As Berman notes, there has long been an expectation that photojournalists can document in public without any restrictions on their work. This is because legally, in the US, everyone has that right. As this debate has unfolded, many photojournalists have insisted that in addition to their legal protections, uncensored documentation is a cornerstone of journalistic endeavor. As veteran photographer David Burnett put it, "Anything which gives away even the slightest freedom of observation is a detriment to both journalism, and society as a whole."[26] But not everyone in the field agrees, pitting a newer perspective of "do no harm" (strongly advocating for obtaining consent in public) against a more traditional approach.[27] Berman occupies a middle ground, sensitive to her legal rights and open to new modes of coverage.

The shifting nature of photojournalism itself and what constitutes responsible practice isn't confined to questions of consent. Photographer Patience Zalanga [Chapter 3] pushes back against the established model of "neutral" journalism, advocating for captions that go beyond a traditional Who/What/Where/When and give, for example, greater historical context (see pages 43-44 for her critique of the term "looters"). Her thinking resonates with a growing body of literature on "peace journalism," in which scholars point out that mainstream media, in their reportage on any single event, don't typically tackle the longer-term social structures that led to the event. As Jake Lynch, former Director of the Centre for Peace and Conflict Studies at the University of Sydney, states, "By excluding or downplaying backgrounds and contexts, [the media] privileges dispositional—often essentialist—explanations for people's behavior in conflict over situationist ones."[28] Specifically on coverage of crime or violent actions (such as Zalanga's example of looting), writer Ibrahim Seaga Shaw observes that it is more difficult to notice, and thereby less common to cover, unseen violence like structural racism or social oppression, than to document what happens more overtly.[29] The question of how to make visible a historical and systematized problem like racism in the US is a concern taken up in the forthcoming pages.

/   **The Individual Behind the Lens**

Does identity shape one's visual output? *New York Times* photo editor Brent Lewis has said, "when trying to cover stories in the vein of black life, you probably should have someone who actually lived it. You need to have insight from someone who understands that realm."[30] Photographer and writer Tara Pixley and her colleague Christina Aushana, a photo scholar, add a historical evaluation, looking back to the beginnings of the camera and the kinds of photos that depicted American slaves:

> [E]arly photographers did not innocently or objectively document the "truth" of chattel slavery, but rather participated in the visual culture of American enslavement by staging photographic visions (and social fictions) of racial hierarchy: slave owners commissioned photographers to produce daguerreotype portraits of their slaves.[31]

The white supremacist perspective of those early photographers molded their output and, by extension, shaped our visual historical record.

So should the public know the racial identity of the photographer? Addressing photojournalism in contemporary America, Zalanga, for one, answers yes: "My identity as a Black woman is something that I do want people to know when they are looking at my photographs, because whether I'm documenting Black people, or especially when I'm documenting white people, knowing who I am as a Black woman behind the lens, means understanding a little more of the moment."

Others interviewed offer differing takes, or point to practical considerations as well. Danese Kenon, Director of Video and Photography at the *Philadelphia Inquirer*, for instance, says [in Chapter 7], "If I'm assigning, I'm not just keeping identity in mind; I'm also thinking about people's schedules, who is available to cover a story when we need it photographed." For her, identity matters but is not the only or presiding factor informing photojournalistic work.

/ **Does Diversity Matter?**

US newsrooms remain, to this day, wildly undiversified. To give a few statistics: more than three-quarters of all newsroom employees are white, and over 60% are male.[32] The numbers are even more disturbing in terms of newsroom leadership (for instance, editor positions). According to a 2019 report by the News Leaders Association, minorities comprise just 19.14% of leadership positions in journalism, and when factoring for both ethnicity and gender, the percentages drop further. Black women occupy just 3.04% of all newsroom leadership roles.[33] Danese Kenon puts it simply in her interview: "[T]o my knowledge, there are maybe four Black women, including myself, who are DoPs [Directors of Photography] in some form of a traditional newsroom in the entire country."

Perhaps the better version of my subhead question is: how and why does diversity matter? This is tackled across the interviews, and it's not a topic that exists in a vacuum. Rather, it's a question that has answers regarding access, safety, sensitivity, experience, history, audience, and quality journalism. At many papers, for instance, the diversity of the newsroom does not map to the demographics of the subscribing audience. Per a 2018 report, the *Wall Street Journal* has an 80% white newsroom and a 61% white audience, while the *Morning Call*, a newspaper in Pennsylvania, has a 95% white newsroom and a 38% white audience.[34] Kainaz Amaria, Visuals Editor at *Vox*, believes such imbalances absolutely have impact. Talking specifically about visual news, she says, "Representation in photojournalism is critical, because those who control our news imagery control our collective visual narrative."[35] MaryAnne Golon [Chapter 8], Director of Photography at the *Washington Post*, also addresses this topic in her interview, succinctly stating that "[y]ou go no place but up" with a more diverse newsroom.

/ **Physical Health and Emotional Safety**

The most obvious 2020 safety hazard was Covid-19 itself: how to safely cover a virus when one doesn't even understand what it is or how it works? It's a horror movie with an invisible enemy. This was the situation that photojournalists and editors faced for much of 2020, and it is addressed in almost every single interview, so potent was the experience for journalists trying to document this story. Accordingly, the interviewees talk, for example, about PPE [personal protective equipment], sanitizing their camera equipment, and their fears of getting sick or being too close to chemical disinfectant fumes. In one case, a photographer admits that he was too cavalier in the beginning of the pandemic.

On another level, interviewees describe the psychological and emotional fatigue of documenting a crisis that has no end in sight. It's a weariness that feels inescapable. Added to this was the concern for some that their exposure could put their family at risk, too. Talking specifically about the toll of covering so much death, photographer Abd says, "sometimes it's really hard; it's very difficult to sleep, to get away from those emotions." Kenon, from her perspective as DoP, adds, "This has been a physically grueling year for the newsroom. It has also been a very traumatizing year." That anxiety was attached to each of 2020's two biggest stories and plenty of times collided across the stories, for example, when photographers covering BLM protests—mass gatherings in a moment that called for extreme isolation—worried about catching Covid. The media's exposure to trauma was real.

War correspondents are known to suffer post-traumatic stress disorder (PTSD) at rates equivalent to soldiers in active combat, a theme explored extensively in *Conversations on Conflict Photography*. But it is incredibly important to recognize that journalists can suffer anxiety and depression even when covering stories that occur far from traditional battlefields. In a piece describing the trauma experienced by journalists reporting on Covid, Olivia Messer, a reporter, writes hauntingly: "[T]he isolation of the pandemic had me convinced that my experience of drowning was unique."[36] What she learns, ultimately, is that the phenomenon is widespread.

Many of those interviewed here were covering not one but both of 2020's major crises. In terms of her Black Lives Matter work, Zalanga describes an experience of delayed emotional impact: "It wasn't until several days into the protests that it hit me." The sheer weight of Floyd's death, the import of this murder, tumbled down upon her as she stood alone and watched aerial footage of Minneapolis. Speaking in early 2021, as she recalls the stress and psychological exhaustion of the prior year, she adds, "We are getting closer each day to the trial of Derek Chauvin…I have time to prepare for my own self-care."

/   Threats Against the Press

Zalanga's stress also stemmed from concerns for her physical safety. The protests not only brought out supporters of the Black Lives Matter cause, but also white supremacists. Unfortunately, 2020 witnessed new levels of threats against journalists, particularly journalists of color.[37] As Zalanga says pointedly, "I can take my camera gear off, so you don't know I'm a journalist. But I can't take my skin off. I'm still Black."

What was *not* new to 2020 was rhetoric against journalists. In the American context, this has been well documented, with a spike in such language as former President Donald Trump entered the political arena. He had a perilously antagonistic relationship with the press, particularly press that was critical of him, and he often referred to media correspondents as the "enemy of the people," a phrase that stands directly in opposition to the fundamental role of journalism in a democracy. CNN's Chief International Anchor, Christiane Amanpour, offered a scathing rebuke: "I cannot tell you how many world leaders use the words 'fake news' to justify their crackdowns. If it's a good enough bludgeon for the President of the United States, it's more than good enough for us, they reason."[38]

While such language has had dreadful ramifications around the globe, it has also reverberated in the US, where it was first spoken. Trump's rhetoric fostered a more dangerous climate for American journalists by emboldening ordinary people to harass representatives of the press. Kenon, for example, gives a terrifying description of multiple photographers in her department being attacked while they worked. As she states quite candidly, "I do remember worrying that our people are not prepared for this if it gets violent."

In 2020, for the first time in its history, the International Crisis Group, an independent non-governmental organization whose mission is to call attention ahead of deadly conflicts in hot spots around the globe, warned of the risk of political violence in America.[39] The Committee to Protect Journalists, in an end-of-year report, likewise noted "unprecedented attacks" against American journalists.[40] The country's highly polarized political terrain, the militarization of law enforcement at protests, and the vast spread of disinformation have all contributed to an incredibly dangerous moment in journalistic history.

JOURNALISM TODAY AND TOMORROW

The many ethical and safety concerns addressed here in brief are elaborated upon through the experiences of the photojournalists and photo editors whose interviews comprise the following pages. In the US, these myriad challenges gained in momentum and ricocheted down a pathway that led to January 6.

Figure 1.4   /   Pro-Trump rioters vandalize equipment belonging to Associated Press journalists outside the Capitol Building, January 6, 2021.

© Christopher Lee for *Time*

But the extraordinary challenges of 2020 exist much more broadly than just in the US. Reporters Without Borders says that the coming years will be make or break for journalism around the world, as we are facing "a geopolitical crisis (due to the aggressiveness of authoritarian regimes); a technological crisis (due to a lack of democratic guarantees); a democratic crisis (due to polarisation and repressive policies); a crisis of trust (due to suspicion and even hatred of the media); and an economic crisis (impoverishing quality journalism)."[41]

With over 1.4 trillion images created on a yearly basis these days, there is no denying the prodigious role that photos play in our lives, as modes of communication and documentation, and, without question, in the distribution and consumption of current events.

This collection aims to better inform the public of the inner workings of this vital mode of journalism, in the hope that the coming years will not be so dire. When the public understands, the public cares more. In caring more for the free press, we demand more of it. We hold journalism to high expectations—as we should. And we also support journalism. It is fundamental to a functioning democracy. That benefits all of us. As Shashi Tharoor, an Indian politician, writer, and former Under-Secretary-General for the United Nations, has said, "Freedom of the press is the mortar that binds together the bricks of democracy."[42]

— Lauren Walsh
NYC
June 2021

NOTES

1   For instance, see Dan Barry, Mike McIntire, and Matthew Rosenberg, "'Our President Wants Us Here': The Mob That Stormed the Capitol," *New York Times*, January 9, 2021, https://www.nytimes.com/2021/01/09/us/capitol-rioters.html; Gabrielle Gurley, "This, Too, Is America," *American Prospect*, January 18, 2021, https://prospect.org/politics/this-too-is-america/; and Edward Lempinen, "The old guard and Trumpism are at war. Can the GOP survive?" *Berkeley News*, February 12, 2021, https://news.berkeley.edu/2021/02/12/the-old-guard-and-trumpism-are-at-war-can-the-gop-survive/. For a piece on the trending of #CivilWar on Twitter, see Alyssa Therrien, "'Civil War' trends on Twitter as Trump supporters storm US Capitol," *Daily Hive*, January 6, 2021, https://dailyhive.com/vancouver/washington-trump-civil-war-trending-twitter.

2   See, for instance, Rebecca Heilweil and Shirin Ghaffary, "How Trump's internet built and broadcast the Capitol insurrection," Recode by *Vox*, January 8, 2021, https://www.vox.com/recode/22221285/trump-online-capitol-riot-far-right-parler-twitter-facebook, and Brandy Zadrozny and Ben Collins, "Violent threats ripple through far-right internet forums ahead of protest," NBCNews.com, January 5, 2021, https://www.nbcnews.com/tech/internet/violent-threats-ripple-through-far-right-internet-forums-ahead-protest-n1252923.

3   For example, see Mary Clare Jalonick and Lisa Mascaro, "GOP blocks Capitol riot probe, displaying loyalty to Trump," AP News, May 28, 2021, https://apnews.com/article/michael-pence-donald-trump-capitol-siege-government-and-politics-4798a8617bacf27bbb576a4b805b85d9; Morgan Chalfant, "White

House: Biden 'remains committed' to Jan. 6 probe," *The Hill*, May 28, 2021, https://thehill.com/homenews/administration/555988-white-house-biden-remains-committed-to-jan-6-probe; and Lois Beckett and Joan E. Greve, "Manchin criticizes Republican opposition to 6 January commission: 'There's no excuse'—as it happened," *The Guardian*, May 27, 2021, https://www.theguardian.com/us-news/live/2021/may/27/joe-biden-republicans-covid-coronavirus-us-politics-latest-updates.

4   See Maneesh Arora, "How the coronavirus pandemic helped the Floyd protests become the biggest in US history," *Washington Post*, August 5, 2020, https://www.washingtonpost.com/politics/2020/08/05/how-coronavirus-pandemic-helped-floyd-protests-become-biggest-us-history/. Black Lives Matter, a sociopolitical movement, predates 2020. The hashtag #BlackLivesMatter first appeared on social media in response to the acquittal of George Zimmerman in the shooting death of Black teenager Trayvon Martin in 2013. The movement gained in momentum after the deaths of Michael Brown in Ferguson, Missouri, and Eric Garner in New York City in 2014.

5   See Marco Aquino and Marcelo Rochabrun, "Peru revises pandemic death toll, now worst in the world per capita," Reuters, June 1, 2021, https://www.reuters.com/world/americas/peru-almost-triples-official-covid-19-death-toll-after-review-180000-2021-05-31/.

6   In April 2021, Chauvin was convicted of second-degree unintentional murder, third-degree murder, and second-degree manslaughter in the death of Floyd. President Joseph Biden, Jr. noted the extraordinary rarity of this conviction. Few American officers are charged with murder in deaths that occur while in the line of duty, and only a small fraction of those charged are convicted. This situation has led to a widespread feeling that white officers kill Black individuals with impunity. In June 2021, Chauvin was sentenced to twenty-two-and-a-half years in prison.

7   See Maneesh Arora, "How the coronavirus pandemic helped," *Washington Post*, August 5, 2020. The video of Floyd's death was recorded with a cell phone by Darnella Frazier, who was seventeen at the time.

8   See Michael T. Heaney, "The George Floyd protests generated more media coverage than any protest in 50 years," *Washington Post*, July 6, 2020, https://www.washingtonpost.com/politics/2020/07/06/george-floyd-protests-generated-more-media-coverage-than-any-protest-50-years/.

9   See Aleem Maqbool, "Black Lives Matter: From social media post to global movement," BBC News (website). July 10, 2020, https://www.bbc.com/news/world-us-canada-53273381 and James Poniewozik, "As the Chauvin Trial Closes, Will Seeing Be Believing?" *New York Times*, April 19, 2021, https://www.nytimes.com/2021/04/19/arts/television/chauvin-trial-video.html.

10 See Abigail Haworth, "The Global Fight for Black Lives, *Marie Claire*, November 23, 2020, https://www.marieclaire.com/politics/a34515361/black-lives-matter-international/.

11 See Michael Birnbaum, "Black Lives Matter protesters in Belgium want statues of colonialist King Léopold II to come down," *Washington Post*, June 9, 2020, https://www.washingtonpost.com/world/europe/black-lives-matter-protests-king-leopold-statues/2020/06/09/042039f6-a9c5-11ea-9063-e69bd6520940_story.html. King Léopold II of Belgium, who reigned from 1865 to 1909, was the owner and absolute ruler of the Congo Free State, which was a private mercenary project. The king made a fortune, as local inhabitants were forced into labor to collect ivory and harvest natural rubber. This colonial project was characterized by endemic brutality, including mass torture and murder. Millions of Congolese died, and the term "crimes against humanity" is thought to have been first used in description of the barbaric practices instituted during Léopold's administration of the state.

12 See Edmund Ruge, "Black Lives Matter Protest Gathers Hundreds at Rio Governor's Palace," RioOnWatch, June 1, 2020, https://rioonwatch.org/?p=59984.

13 See John Campbell, "Black Lives Matter Protests in Africa Shine a Light on Local Police Brutality," Council on Foreign Relations (website), July 8, 2020, https://www.cfr.org/blog/black-lives-matter-protests-africa-shine-light-local-police-brutality.

14 For instance, see Berkeley Lovelace Jr., Jasmine Kim, and Will Feuer, "WHO walks back comments on asymptomatic coronavirus spread, says much is still unknown," CNBC.com, June 9, 2020, https://www.cnbc.com/2020/06/09/who-scrambles-to-clarify-comments-on-asymptomatic-coronavirus-spread-much-is-still-unknown.html and Tim Elfrink, Ben Guarino, and Chris Mooney, "CDC reverses itself and says guidelines it posted on coronavirus airborne transmission were wrong," *Washington Post*, September 21, 2020, https://www.washingtonpost.com/nation/2020/09/21/cdc-covid-aerosols-airborne-guidelines/.

15 See "2021 World Press Freedom Index: Journalism, the vaccine against disinformation, blocked in more than 130 countries," Reporters Without Borders (website), April 17, 2021, https://rsf.org/en/2021-world-press-freedom-index-journalism-vaccine-against-disinformation-blocked-more-130-countries.

16 Excess mortality is an epidemiological concept that accounts for deaths above what is expected in "normal" times. On excess death in Peru, see Luke Taylor, "Covid-19: Why Peru suffers from one of the highest excess death rates in the world," *BMJ*, March 9, 2021, https://www.bmj.com/content/372/bmj.n611, as well as the first chart in Charlie Giattino, Hannah Ritchie, Max Roser, Esteban Ortiz-Ospina, and Joe Hassell, "Excess mortality during the coronavirus pandemic (Covid-19)," Our World in Data (website), as of June 6, 2021, https://ourworldindata.org/excess-mortality-covid. In June 2021, it became clear that the government had been under-reporting its country's death toll, when a revised system for tallying Covid mortalities more than doubled Peru's official toll. For more on under-reporting and/or healthcare failures, see Luis Felipe López-Calva, "A greater tragedy than we know: Excess mortality rates suggest that Covid-19 death toll is vastly underestimated in LAC," UNDP: Latin America and the Caribbean (website), July 7, 2020, https://www.latinamerica.undp.org/content/rblac/en/home/presscenter/director-s-graph-for-thought/a-greater-tragedy-than-we-know--excess-mortality-rates-suggest-t.html, and Simeon Tegel, "Peru's Covid crisis: 'Almost all Peruvians know someone who died,'" Al Jazeera, May 6, 2021, https://www.aljazeera.com/news/2021/5/6/perus-covid-crisis-almost-all-peruvians-know-someone-who-died. Of note, "Peruvians had long suspected they weren't getting the true picture" in terms of the nation's Covid mortality rates. See "Covid: Peru more than doubles death toll after review," BBC News (website), June 1, 2021, https://www.bbc.com/news/world-latin-america-57307861.

17 Although many suspected the government's announced Covid numbers were too low, the "Ministry [of Justice and Human Rights] urged people to share only official information, accompanied by the hashtag 'Don't Spread #FakeNews.'" Meanwhile, "Peru became the first country in Latin America to implement prison sentences for creating and disseminating fake news" with regard to the pandemic. Alvarez-Risco et al, "The Peru Approach against the COVID-19 Infodemic: Insights and Strategies," in the *American Journal of Tropical Medicine and Hygiene*, Vol 103(2) 583-86, published online June 2020, https://www.ncbi.nlm.nih.gov/pmc/articles/PMC7410469/#b28. See also notes 5, 6, and 7 in the Abd interview on press freedom concerns in Peru.

18 See Christopher Torchia, "Pandemic's toll among journalists in Peru is especially high," AP News, August 20, 2020, https://apnews.com/article/9b435c25a06906b71a4ca902972ee890.

19 See, for instance, Beina Xu and Eleanor Albert, "Media Censorship in China," Council on Foreign Relations (website), February 17, 2017, https://www.cfr.org/backgrounder/media-censorship-china; Alex Matthews with Edward Yang, "China's lack of press freedom causes problems for the world," Deutsche Welle, April 21, 2020, https://www.dw.com/en/chinas-lack-of-press-freedom-causes-problems-for-the-world/a-53198195; and "One Country, One Censor: How China undermines media freedom in Hong Kong and Taiwan," Committee to Protect Journalists (website), December 16, 2019, https://cpj.org/reports/2019/12/one-country-one-censor-china-hong-kong-taiwan-press-freedom/.

20 See "2021 World Press Freedom Index," Reporters Without Borders (website), April 17, 2021.

21 See Peter Maass, "Hiding Covid-19: How the Trump Administration Suppresses Photography of the Pandemic," The Intercept, December 27, 2020, https://theintercept.com/2020/12/27/covid-photography-hospitals/.

22 See Lauren Egan, "Trump calls coronavirus Democrats' 'new hoax,'" NBCNews.com, February 28, 2020, https://www.nbcnews.com/politics/donald-trump/trump-calls-coronavirus-democrats-new-hoax-n1145721. For an example of how this thinking continued months later, see, for instance, Chris McGreal, "'It's a hoax. There's no pandemic': Trump's base stays loyal as president fights Covid," *The Guardian*, October 3, 2020, https://www.theguardian.com/us-news/2020/oct/03/donald-trump-base-stays-loyal-president-fights-covid-19.

23 See Sarah Elizabeth Lewis, "Where Are the Photos of People Dying of Covid?" *New York Times*, May 1, 2020, https://www.nytimes.com/2020/05/01/opinion/coronavirus-photography.html.

24 See, for instance, the Introduction to Lauren Walsh, *Conversations on Conflict Photography* (London: Routledge, 2019), xi-xxi, for discussion of Western reaction to "faraway" suffering. For a focus on the imbalances in how newsrooms handle graphic imagery depending on whether the photographic subject is foreign or local, see Helen Lewis, "How Newsrooms Handle Graphic Images of Violence," *Nieman Reports*, January 5, 2016, https://niemanreports.org/articles/how-newsrooms-handle-graphic-images-of-violence/.

25 See, for instance, Kelly McBride, "Should Images Of Protesters Be Blurred To Protect Them From Retribution?" KGOU.org, June 18, 2020, https://www.kgou.org/post/should-images-protesters-be-blurred-protect-them-retribution, and Brent Lewis, "Blurring Faces Is Anti-Journalistic and Anti-Human," *Wired*, June 30, 2020, https://www.wired.com/story/opinion-blurring-faces-is-anti-journalistic-and-anti-human/, as well as note 2 in the Berman interview.

26 See David Burnett, "An Open Letter to the NPPA on Ethics," PetaPixel (website), July 7, 2020, https://petapixel.com/2020/07/07/david-burnett-an-open-letter-to-the-nppa-on-ethics/.

27 See Eliana Miller and Nicole Asbury, "Photographers are being called on to stop showing protesters' faces. Should they?" Poynter Institute (website), June 4, 2020, https://www.poynter.org/ethics-trust/2020/should-journalists-show-protesters-faces/. For more on "do no harm" photography, see: Authority Collective, "Do No Harm: Photographing Police Brutality Protests," press release/open letter, May 31, 2020, https://drive.google.com/file/d/1hFvB_cGM_TfVVNuXV-Jg6mO4DIPLvNoC/view.

28 Quoted in Ibrahim Seaga Shaw, Jake Lynch, and Robert A. Hackett (eds.), *Expanding Peace Journalism* (Sydney: Sydney University Press, 2011), 97-98.

29 Ibid. Shaw critiques this kind of journalism and advocates for deeper contextualization of underlying social conditions in order to support peace-building processes.

30 Quoted in Tara Pixley, "Why We Need More Visual Journalists and Editors of Color," *Nieman Reports*, May 15, 2017, https://niemanreports.org/articles/a-new-focus/.

31 See Christina Aushana and Tara Pixley, "Protest Photography Can Be a Powerful Tool For and Against Black Lives Matter," *Nieman Reports*, July 13, 2020, https://niemanreports.org/articles/protest-photography-and-black-lives-matter/.

32 See Elizabeth Grieco, "Newsroom employees are less diverse than US employees overall," Pew Research Center (website), November 2, 2018, https://www.pewresearch.org/fact-tank/2018/11/02/newsroom-employees-are-less-diverse-than-u-s-workers-overall/.

33 See Meredith D. Clark, et al, "2019 ASNE Diversity Survey: Detailed Tables," NewsLeaders.org (website), September 10, 2019, https://static1.squarespace.com/static/5d2df6a6231a750001881b75/t/5d76c698c87c4c7550640ec2/1568065177406/Summary+Tables+2019_9.6.19.pdf. More information about the 2019 ASNE Diversity Survey can be found here: https://www.newsleaders.org/2019-diversity-survey-results.

34 See the 2018 results in American Society of News Editors, "How Diverse Are US Newsrooms?" American Community Survey/ASNE, Census 2011–15, https://googletrends.github.io/asne/?view=4.

35 See Sahar Amer, "Diverse storytelling enhances your journalism," Reuters, September 20, 2019, https://www.reutersagency.com/en/reuters-community/the-importance-of-strong-diverse-photojournalism/.

36 See Olivia Messer, "The COVID Reporters Are Not Okay. Extremely Not Okay." Study Hall (website), May 6, 2021, https://studyhall.xyz/the-reporters-are-not-okay-extremely-not-okay/.

37 See Courtney Douglas, "Amid Black Lives Matter protests, a crushing moment for journalists facing record attacks, arrests at the hands of law enforcement," Reporters Committee for Freedom of the Press (website), September 4, 2020, https://www.rcfp.org/black-lives-matter-press-freedom/, and Elahe Izadi and Paul Farhi, "'The terror of wearing both a press badge and black skin': Black journalists are carrying unique burdens," *Washington Post*, June 1, 2020, https://www.washingtonpost.com/lifestyle/media/the-terror-of-wearing-both-a-press-badge-and-black-skin-black-journalists-are-carrying-unique-burdens-right-now/2020/06/01/2266a258-a414-11ea-b473-04905b1af82b_story.html.

38 See Christiane Amanpour's testimony at the hearing on "Human Rights at Home: Media, Politics, and the Safety of Journalists," US Committee on Security and Cooperation in Europe, delivered July 23, 2020, https://www.csce.gov/sites/helsinkicommission.house.gov/files/Testimony%20of%20Christiane%20Amanpour.pdf.

39 Robert Malley, "Crisis Group Turns Focus to Risk of Electoral Violence in the US," International Crisis Group (website), October 2, 2020, https://www.crisisgroup.org/content/crisis-group-turns-focus-risk-electoral-violence-us.

40 See Katherine Jacobsen, "In 2020, US journalists faced unprecedented attacks," Committee to Protect Journalists (website), December 14, 2020, https://cpj.org/2020/12/in-2020-u-s-journalists-faced-unprecedented-attacks/. For information on journalists targeted specifically by US police, see Marc Tracy and Rachel Abrams, "Police Target Journalists as Trump Blames 'Lamestream Media,' for Protests," *New York Times*, June 1, 2020, https://www.nytimes.com/2020/06/01/business/media/reporters-protests-george-floyd.html; Tracy Brown, "As Trump blames 'lamestream media,' journalists arrested and injured during protests," *Los Angeles Times*, June 1, 2020, https://www.latimes.com/entertainment-arts/story/2020-06-01/journalists-attacked-arrested-george-floyd-protest-coverage; and "Daily Briefing: Some journalists arrested, injured by police during protests," Pew Research Center (website), June 1, 2020, https://www.journalism.org/daily-briefings/2020/06/01/some-journalists-arrested-injured-by-police-during-protests/.

41 See "2021 World Press Freedom Index," Reporters Without Borders (website), April 17, 2021.

42 From comments given at UN Headquarters in observance of World Press Freedom Day, May 3, 2001.

A NOTE
ON THE INTERVIEWS

The interviews in *Through the Lens* were conducted in person, via phone, or via Zoom, between fall 2020 and February 2021, with updates as needed before publication. Each has been condensed and edited for clarity and grammar. When it seemed necessary, I also endeavored to contextualize (via endnotes) references made to people, places, historical events, and discipline-specific terminology.

The interview with Aly Song was conducted with live, simultaneous translation by Richard Chen and Vivian Xing.

INTERVIEWS WITH

US-BASED PHOTOJOURNALISTS

2 NINA BERMAN

NINA BERMAN is an American photographer who covered the conflict in Bosnia and Taliban-ruled Afghanistan in the late 1990s. She now focuses attention on the aftermath of war and contemporary political and social landscapes in the US. Her photographs and videos have been exhibited at over one hundred venues world-wide, including the Whitney Museum of American Art in New York, the Museum of Fine Arts, Houston, the Zachęta National Gallery of Art in Poland, and Dublin Contemporary.

Berman has received awards from the New York Foundation for the Arts, the Open Society Foundations, World Press Photo, and Hasselblad, among others. She is a professor at Columbia University Graduate School of Journalism and a 2021 Knight Science Journalism Fellow at MIT (Massachusetts Institute of Technology).

LAUREN WALSH / During Black Lives Matter protests in the US, some people demanded that photojournalists stop photographing protesters, or that they not distribute those images or that they blur the faces of protesters. The concern is that by putting the images out and making protesters identifiable, the individuals in the photo are at risk, for instance, of police retaliation. What is your take on this?

NINA BERMAN / Prior to this 2020 conversation, there was a strong consensus that with protests, and really any activities in public, journalists didn't need to ask consent of people they were photographing because there is no expectation of privacy when someone is out on the street at a political event. And to ask consent is antithetical to what journalists are supposed to do, which is to witness and document.

Now this view is being called into question, and I and others are reflecting on it, because of the use of facial recognition technology, and because of the perception, valid or not, that police are using images made by professional photojournalists to aid in the arrest or surveillance of protesters.[2] So even though I have been in situations where protesters may scream at me or other journalists to stop photographing—while they're taking their own pictures and live-streaming their presence, which seems completely hypocritical—I feel I have to meet people where they are, and understand their headspace.

So I have become more cautious. If I am going to take a picture of someone at a Black Lives Matter protest, where that person is the dominant element in the frame and I am close to them, I will ask them, "Do you mind if I photograph you?" or will seek some non-verbal sign that they're okay with me taking pictures. As a result, I may lose some degree of spontaneity. However, most protests are choreographed performances, anyway. To think that all of these moments exist unscripted is not really to accept the reality of how these events operate.

LW / So if you don't get consent from a protester, would you drop the image or would you try to photograph the same scene, but in a different way that would protect identities?

NB / Let me give you a hypothetical: If the police had just killed someone and I'm there to make a picture of the emotional aftermath, and someone says, "Don't take my picture" and they are really insistent about it, then I will try to avoid including that person in the frame. Legally, I can take that photo and that person has no legitimate standing to keep me from working in a public space, but I feel that ethically as a journalist, I have to understand the fears and sensitivities of the people that I'm covering. This holds for people who are not in positions of power. Obviously, if I saw police officers beating someone, I would not stop to ask the officers if I could take their picture. And if a public official asked me to stop photographing while in a public place, I wouldn't be inclined to comply.

But as for blurring faces, I don't think that's a solution. This blurred photo [Figure 2.2] is ridiculous—and was meant to be; it's an exercise in visual absurdity. Can you imagine a world where protesters have no expressions or individuality? I'm not interested in photography that blurs away the outrage of a public uprising. This is a moment of mass action.

Figures 2.1 and 2.2 / Black Lives Matter protesters in New York City, June 2, 2020. The version of the photo that appears on the right was created by Berman to illustrate her point that blurring diminishes the image.

© Nina Berman

What drew me to this moment [Figure 2.1] was the diversity of the crowd and the expressions on their faces—the emotion and the solidarity, as they took to the street. The Black Power salute that you see in the photo connects the past with the present, signifying that what we are witnessing today is a continuation of a longstanding struggle.[3] There is a history behind today's events. In photojournalism, you're looking for those elements, those gestures that carry across times.

No one told me not to photograph in that moment. But if a bunch of people start screaming at me "Don't take my picture!" then I will find another way to document, or will move on to a different group. I feel that this is a time for us photographers to reflect on our practice and work harder at building trust.

LW / Have you been in a situation like that, where you had to find another way to make the picture?

NB / Sure, for instance, over the summer I was covering a Black Lives Matter event at the mayor's home at Gracie Mansion [in New York City]. There were maybe 700 people there. Before the event kicked off, the protest leader told a few of us that pictures of people's faces were forbidden. The AP and the *New York Times* photographers walked away and refused to even acknowledge the statement. I tried to talk with the person to understand why, and he flipped me off. But I took it as a kind of challenge: Could I cover this in another way? What would

Figure 2.3 / Black Lives Matter protesters in New York City, June 3, 2020.

that photography look like? I ended up being a far less aggressive, in-your-face photographer. I was more sensitive to the temperature of the crowd, and my photography became much quieter. My pictures, in turn, were more selective.

This photo [Figure 2.3], which is from the protest at Gracie Mansion, is a way to show the size of the crowd and the unity of purpose without showing faces. Hopefully you feel the solidarity in the gesture of the raised arms, serving as stand-ins for the faces, which one doesn't see but is encouraged to imagine. The composition and perspective here is one often used by photo-journalists, but frequently for a secondary photo; in this case, this image was *the* central picture to document and convey this event.

LW / Speaking of "quieter" or subtler imagery, this [Figure 2.4] isn't a typical portrayal of Covid, where it is more common to see face masks or gloves. Yet you have captioned this as a pandemic image. What do you hope the viewer sees or understands?

NB / A lot of things were going on in my mind when I made that picture. That graphic had been put up before the pandemic. It's about family separation and ICE [Immigration and Customs Enforcement] policies.[4] That was the initial reference of that graphic.

One thing that Covid did to everybody was separate them from their families. You couldn't travel, couldn't see people that you loved, couldn't visit your parents, and so forth. That loss of connection and that separation from family was now felt by people with full citizenship, who maybe never before had to think about what it meant to not be able to see a loved one. I'm not saying that Covid separation is equivalent to the threats and fears experienced by those incarcerated or facing deportation, but on an existential level, the pandemic provided a point of comparison. So I developed a more intense compassion and empathy for people who live this situation or this threat all the time because of US policies.

Alongside that thinking was the fact that I had photographed quite a lot of protests against ICE actions. There was a focus on that in New York City in the pre-pandemic months, but then those protests took a big hit, with people not being able to go out on the street because of Covid. So the devastation of Covid isn't isolated to the medical world. It's so much bigger; it bleeds out and has impact on social movements and connects with political policies. All of those things were merging in my mind when I took this picture and I think it resonates beyond the graphic's initial intention.

LW / Are we generally lacking in those visuals that, in layered fashion, bring Covid together with other ongoing sociopolitical matters in the United States?

NB / I think most photographers don't think in terms of such intersectionality when they're making pictures. I think that's true generally, that images of intersectionality tend to be fewer than, say, the dramatic news image or the one-dimensional cliché image. In a horrific news event, like a pandemic, with mass death, photographers are trying to show evidence that this is happening: people on stretchers, dying from Covid; refrigerator trucks [which were used out-side hospitals as temporary morgues] all over New York City. And so the quieter, intersectional

Figure 2.4 / A street scene with a sign supporting family reunification for immigrants separated by federal authorities. Social distancing during the pandemic hurt the ability of activists to make their voices heard. New York City, April 1, 2020.

© Nina Berman

picture, which won't get as much play, is not going to be a priority for most photographers, especially those working news beats.

As Covid cases surged in the US, all of a sudden there were so many of those dramatic photos. In turn, photographers have left a lot of space for other kinds of more metaphorical imagery. So I like this photo that fuses family separation with the Covid moment because I felt like it was different from the other pictures out there.

Whether we need more pictures like that, well, I don't know how many people actually appreciate that kind of photo. But in a perfect set-up we would have space for all of it—the images on one topic and the images connecting topics. Pictures that are not just looking at a particular event or time can function beyond the moment and can help you see more broadly and understand in new ways.

LW / Regarding some of your Covid imagery, did you find it challenging to create pictures that capture some kind of essential humanity or that inspire empathy in the viewer when you can't see the face of the subject, because with so much Covid photography, people are masked or shielded or have goggles? It is, frankly, hard to see who they are.

Figure 2.5 / Healthcare workers, including nurses and paramedics, respond to the 7:00 p.m. clap by firefighters and New Yorkers honoring them, NYU Langone Hospital, New York City, April 4, 2020.

© Nina Berman

NB /   Well, I photographed many events organized by nurses, and one particular thing I wanted to experience and photograph was the 7:00 p.m. clap because it was such a unique thing.[5] You look at this photo [Figure 2.5] and there is something about that shield, something almost angelic. I felt this when I saw that moment. It felt very theatrical. This particular picture is shot with a long lens, and the context is stripped away; but there was something about the gesture that seemed almost religious.

When you can't see faces, you have to look at the moment another way. Often you want to capture someone's eyes; they're expressive. Here, I couldn't do that, but I think the gesture itself is revealing. Is she holding her hands up for help, or praying? In actuality, she is clapping but I caught her frozen before her hands meet. So then the photo becomes something more than that specific moment; it's something essential about this greater moment in history.

At a visual level this occurs because the woman is isolated; it's just her gesture with a black background. This could be anywhere. It becomes representative of the experience, not of the one person we are looking at. In that sense, it's lacking in precise context and applies more universally or essentially to the situation of Covid.

LW /   What are the biggest ethical concerns with regard to photojournalistic coverage now?

NB /   For me, personally, I have been thinking about my role in contributing to the visual narratives of these major events of 2020. I don't really feel entitled to cover something if I either don't know it well, or if I'm not going to put in the hard work to learn the landscape. A lot of photographers see themselves as "I'm an image maker. That's what I do. That's all I do." But I make images to communicate ideas and problems.

This has been an interesting moment, especially with Covid, for so many American or European photographers who currently can't travel but who are so used to relying on their passports to traipse around the world, covering faraway places. That's not the way photographers should work.

We [the photojournalistic community] are rethinking the idea of whose pictures tell the story, and paying more attention to who is behind the camera and what that person's lived experience, as opposed to only their photographic ability, brings to the story. This is a big change in the industry and a welcome one. People see differently depending on who they are, the circumstances in which they were raised, their privilege or lack thereof, their class origins, race, gender identity, cultural influences, and on and on. And so if we're going to try to document the world in any kind of meaningful and insightful way, then a diversity of witnesses and creators is essential. What's surprising, when you think of it, is how long it took to get to this moment.

NOTES

1   This interview with Berman was conducted in fall 2020.

2   For various takes on the issue of facial recognition technology and protests, see, for example, Alex
Hodor-Lee (writer) and Nina Berman (photographer), "The blurred faces—and ethics—of protest
photography," June 23, 2020, Document Journal (website),
https://www.documentjournal.com/2020/06/the-blurred-faces-and-ethics-of-protest-photography/,
Malkia Devich-Cyril, "Defund Facial Recognition," *The Atlantic,* July 5, 2020,
https://www.theatlantic.com/technology/archive/2020/07/defund-facial-recognition/613771/, or
Kashmir Hill, "Activists Turn Facial Recognition Tools Against the Police," *New York Times*,
October 21, 2020, https://www.nytimes.com/2020/10/21/technology/facial-recognition-police.html.

3   This salute is represented by an extended, raised arm with the hand balled into a fist. In terms of
photography, this salute was made immortal in a 1968 photo by John Dominis when two Black
American runners, competing in the Olympics in Mexico City, made this gesture as they stood on a
dais after receiving their medals. As *Time* put it, "Their message could not have been clearer: Before
we salute America, America must treat blacks as equal." See "Black Power Salute," in *100
Photographs: The Most Influential Images of All Time* (New York: *Time* Books, 2015), 68.

4   For more on family separation under the Trump administration, see the Platt interview, note 2. Such policies
were implemented by the US Department of Justice and carried out by various agencies, including ICE,
US Customs and Border Protection, and the local law enforcement departments who cooperated with
them. The artwork Berman has documented in this photo is called REUNITE by Ronald Rael and Virginia
San Fratello. It is an open-source, downloadable image intended by the artists for use in child
separation protest events anywhere in the world.

5   In the early weeks of the pandemic in New York City, New Yorkers clapped and cheered every evening
at 7:00 p.m. It was a signal of support to the medical personnel and other essential workers who were
handling Covid while the city was the global hot spot. As one *New York Times* reporter put it, "For many
New Yorkers, the time of coronavirus will be defined by two sounds. One is the ambulance siren. The other
its opposite: the nightly 7 o'clock cheer for front-line workers." See Andy Newman, "What N.Y.C. Sounds Like
Every Night at 7," *New York Times*, April 10, 2020,
https://www.nytimes.com/interactive/2020/04/10/nyregion/nyc-7pm-cheer-thank-you-coronavirus.html.

3   PATIENCE ZALANGA

PATIENCE ZALANGA *is a freelance photojournalist based in Minneapolis–St. Paul, Minnesota. Born in Nigeria, she immigrated to the United States in 1994. Since 2014, her photography has focused primarily on American social movements and uprisings, with an emphasis on the Movement for Black Lives.*

Her work has been featured in numerous outlets, including the New York Times, Time, The Guardian, *Minnesota Public Radio, NPR, Nightline, Upworthy, BuzzFeed News, AJ+, and* Femme Photographes. *In 2020, she won the Walker Art Center's Community Artist Award, and her photograph of an outraged Black Lives Matter protester in Minneapolis made* Time's *"Top 100 Photos of 2020."*

LAUREN WALSH / Your bio notes that you document the Movement for Black Lives. Why is that topic important to you?[1]

PATIENCE ZALANGA / I've had a passion for journalism since I was a kid, always knew I wanted to be a journalist one day. But this particular focus began for me in November of 2014, when I went to Ferguson, Missouri. This was about one week before the grand jury was to make their announcement on whether Darren Wilson, the police officer accused of killing Michael Brown, would be indicted.[2] I didn't initially bring my camera because I was nervous; I was reading about police officers destroying protesters' equipment. I was there as a supporter, and to experience this history as it happened. I didn't go with the intent to document journalistically.

I was there seven days and the announcement didn't occur. It was when I was on my way home that the grand jury declared they would not indict Wilson. I went back the following day, this time with my camera. I knew I needed to document this. I wasn't on any journalistic assignment, and at the time didn't quite realize yet, but this was the beginning of what would shape my work and lay the path into journalism.

It was also the first time I deeply experienced a disconnect between events I was seeing and how they were being covered in the news. So I used social media to give updates. I used it to let people know I was okay, but also Twitter was influential in getting information out, in real time, that contradicted what the police were communicating about situations in Ferguson, about the response from the public to the grand jury's decision to not indict for murder. The police were alleging that protesters were violent, that they were instigating police reactions, but in reality the protesters were peaceful, and this was not being accurately communicated to the public in the news.[3]

Since then, I have been covering this broad topic, Black lives, as an American issue, whether I'm documenting the fiftieth anniversary of Bloody Sunday in Selma, Alabama, or the response to the killing of Jamar Clark [by police] in north Minneapolis in 2015, or the aftermath of the killing of George Floyd here in 2020.[4] This has been an issue for a long time. Many of our political leaders in Minneapolis were warned. Black and Brown people in the city were telling them to be careful well before 2020. They said this will be exponentially worse down the line. And then it was. What happened with Floyd's death was confirmation of what many of us already knew—the gravity of the rage and anger and resentment and distrust of the police in Minneapolis. [See Figure 3.1]

LW / Did it ever feel too close to home? The murder that led to national and international protests happened right where you live.

PZ / At times it was too, too, too close to home. The part of this that made it especially terrifying wasn't the fires, the police, the tear gas; those are components of protests that I've seen. It was the white supremacists. Photographing this time presented a new level of danger for me. I can take my camera gear off, so you don't know I'm a journalist. But I can't take my skin off. I'm still Black. And the threats from white supremacists were very real.[5]

Figure 3.1 / On Instagram, Zalanga captioned this photograph: "To understand what led to May 25th is to acknowledge the deadly legacy of the Minneapolis Police Department. November 15th marked the five year anniversary of Jamar Clark's death. Many people speak on the police killing of George as if it's an isolated incident but the rage had been simmering years prior here in Minneapolis." Image posted to Instagram on November 16, 2020; the photo, from a protest after Clark's killing, was taken on November 16, 2015.

LW / In this sense, your identity puts you at great risk. Are there other ways your identity informs your work or your ability to work?

PZ / Absolutely. Look at this photo, for instance [Figure 3.2]. It's taken on my iPhone. I didn't bring my camera that day. I was struggling with whether I even wanted to continue with photography. I felt like I have taken the same photos, again and again, and I didn't know if what I was doing was actually making any sort of impact or difference, particularly for the Black community.

Figure 3.2 / A woman outraged by the killing of George Floyd speaks to a crowd and blocks a police officer's vehicle in Minneapolis, Minnesota, May 26, 2020.

© Patience Zalanga

When I saw this woman, her outrage and anger really spoke to me in a way that I don't have the words to articulate. But sometimes I see my feelings in other people. They're like a reflection of me, of the feelings I can't quite tap into or communicate.

My identity as a Black woman is something that I do want people to know when they are looking at my photographs, because whether I'm documenting Black people, or especially when I'm documenting white people, knowing who I am as a Black woman behind the lens, means understanding a little more of the moment. The facial expression that you see on the person in the photo may communicate how they see me, too.

Figure 3.3 / Twan reads a book to his son that they got from the Metro Library, a bus shelter that was turned into a free library with books for children. George Floyd Square, Minneapolis, Minnesota, September 26, 2020.

© Patience Zalanga

I've also, at this point, having documented this for years, built a trust or rapport with the community here in Minneapolis. This is crucial because we need to create better context in the documentation, in order to better understand these situations. And you can't do that without learning, gaining trust, getting to know the community. For me, this is about a larger issue of integrity and truth-telling, which means challenging the common visual tropes by documenting the smaller, quieter, subtler moments. You learn how to see those moments the better you know the community.

For instance, this photo [Figure 3.3] is more than a father-son portrait. The two are reading a book they picked together from the free library in George Floyd Square. It might be a moment you would otherwise pass by, but this is an image that challenges the usual perceptions of Black men, particularly in this space that memorializes the violent death of a Black man. This is a tender, quiet interaction, and I hope it deepens the context and invites new perspectives on the Black Lives Matter movement.

LW / Give me an example of where or how context gets lost in other coverage.

PZ / One of the hardest things with photojournalism is the captions. You have the traditional Who, What, Where, When. But nobody really says the Why, to explain what is happening—I mean to really piece it together.

This photo [Figure 3.4] is one in a series I shared that was about what it means to use the word "loot" or to describe people as "looters." What are the implications when Black and Brown people who take things from stores are called looters? What happens when we don't contextualize a longer history—of exploitation, wage theft, land theft in this country? Without talking about these structural harms, we are left with an oversimplified story and that is dangerous.[6]

Large corporations have lost money [from theft or looting], but they bounce back. Who has *really* lost out in this country? When we look back at American history, we realize that the foundation was built on theft of land and life. These things need to be considered and need to be part of the context in how we report. This made it difficult for me to be on assignment [for *Time*], because I felt this is a moment when Black journalists have opportunities like never before, getting jobs with major news organizations, but you have to work within the limits of the system, in this case a system that doesn't want the caption that explains the Why. You have to be objective. You have to be about facts. But then I ask myself: Who gets to decide what is objective? Who gets to say what is neutral? Who gets to say what is factual, or rather which facts matter enough to report?

LW / Do *you* believe journalism should be objective or neutral?

PZ / I can't separate my Blackness from my work, and my Blackness informs how I see the world. It informs how I document moments, and the same should be said about white people who are also within this field. Your whiteness does inform how you see things, how you report the news, what you choose to document. We are all subjective. I'm not saying we should post our personal opinions publicly, but we *should* recognize that our identities inform our work. If you tell yourself you can separate your personal self from your work self, then you never have

patiencezalanga
Minneapolis, Minnesota

· · ·

     ·

850 likes

patiencezalanga It's a part of our collective story but it isn't the only part. I think the part of the story that gets omitted about people breaking into stores is that a lot of the items that were taken was redistributed. Yes, stores were left in shambles, but I think it greatly misses the point. You can't talk about looting without talking about the history of wage theft, land theft and slavery. You can't talk about looting without talking about exploitation. And you definitely can't talk about looting without addressing the murder of George Floyd. My primary concern was that people who did enter these stores would pass out due to smoke inhalation. Thankfully that was not the case. These images were taken on the first couple days of protests in late May.

Figure 3.4 / Zalanga's Instagram post with caption. Photo taken on May 28, 2020.

to reflect on whether your identity influenced your work. Then there is no contemplation about the journalism.

Journalism has not yet really self-reflected on its coverage of race and racism. Many news organizations are working really hard to diversify their newsrooms and to engage in anti-racism work within their fields, but this requires that all people be honest with themselves, and consider their roles and biases and privileges.

I also think we need to reflect on some of the conventions of "objective" journalism. You might read an article that states that President Trump said a number of racist things during his presidency. But you won't read, "President Trump is a racist." Because that is considered subjective. But if he made X number of racist comments, then why isn't he objectively a racist? It's a dance around what is really happening and it does a disservice to the public. It should not be controversial to call someone a racist when they are.

LW / Are race and the pandemic two distinct issues?

PZ / They absolutely overlap. For instance, why are so many people who live near incinerators in Minneapolis getting severely sick from Covid?[7] We have to ask: who lives near the [municipal waste] incinerators? It's a Black neighborhood. So these topics overlap because it's also about geography and environment and class and lack of health care. It's all of the social issues that organizers have, for decades, been fighting for; they all intersect with this pandemic, which amplifies what we already knew existed.

LW / Is it hard, emotionally, to cover so much grief and injustice?

PZ / It is hard, especially when it feels like your home, your community is in danger or your safe places are threatened. [See Figure 3.5]

We are getting closer each day to the trial of [former police officer] Derek Chauvin who stands accused of Floyd's murder.[8] I have time to prepare for my own self-care. What does it look like to check in with myself and to ensure I am getting the rest and care that I need for myself? What is my capacity for this? What happened with me in 2020 was that there was not enough time to process the events in the wake of Floyd's murder because it was all breaking news.

It wasn't until several days into the protests that it hit me. I went to the homeless shelter where I also work. All of the people had been moved to another location. The shelter is in a church that is over 100 years old and my manager, as well as the executive director of the organization, were worried because protesters were setting fires and if there was a fire at the church, it could have been a disaster. People wouldn't escape in time. But I went to the shelter to print my press pass because I do not have a printer at home. The shelter is a safe place for me, but there it was, completely empty. I was standing alone in the living room and the TV was on with an aerial view of south Minneapolis. And I just thought to myself, "this can't be real." It was hitting me. This is what's happening.

Figure 3.5   /   Protesters march down University Avenue in St. Paul, Minnesota, to demand justice for Breonna Taylor, September 23, 2020.[9] On Instagram, Zalanga captioned this image: "Tonight. I close my eyes. And remember. That even in slumber. I am a threat. She was sleeping."

© Patience Zalanga

LW   /   Do you see your photographic work as connected to the visual coverage of the American Civil Rights Movement?

PZ   /   I think the documentation of Black Lives today is an extension of Civil Rights Movement photography. You read writers like James Baldwin and you realize that the language to describe this moment that we are experiencing now has already been written.[10] So what we are doing today as writers and as photographers is updating the progress, or lack thereof. Today's photography can exist independent from the Civil Rights Movement. But when we contextualize what is happening now, these moments connect greatly. I don't think we can or should talk about now without thinking about then. It's a history that reflects the present state of this country.

What's different now is how we consume the images. Will the images from today be remembered like some of the Civil Rights photos from six decades ago? I don't know. There are very impactful photos of Black Lives Matter, but is Instagram, for instance, the best platform? It feels sometimes that it's an inappropriate medium for such intimate work that requires reflection. At the same time, Instagram has been a great equalizer for Black and Brown indigenous visual storytellers, because our images are now seen widely. You have access to people around the world in a way that didn't exist during the 1960s.

LW / Tell me about your recent Polaroid work.

PZ /   So much of the time I have been at George Floyd Square [in Minneapolis], where the memorial [for Floyd] is, has been when I was on assignments. I never really just sat there, for no reason. So I went to experience it differently, and I brought my Polaroid because I wanted another perspective, another view. I went to capture the geography of this space, separate from the people who visit it, the subtle details that often get overlooked. I have pictures of a greenhouse, of signs, of a mural, of a drug needle disposal container.

Figure 3.6 / The gas station Speedway sign at George Floyd Square displays a countdown to the Chauvin trial. January 20, 2021.

© Patience Zalanga

I'm hesitating about whether to post [on Instagram] one photo I took. It's graffiti, on a door in the Square, the number "30" with the letter "Z". It's a Bloods gang sign.[11] Some of the gang members are part of the volunteer groups that provide community security at the Square. I have been trying to figure out what to say about this photo. The Bloods gang presence is part of this space. But how do we talk about that? Who is included in the role of protector? Officials are saying it's time to close the Square and open the streets back up. The Minneapolis Police say this is a dangerous space, a war zone, and these narratives influence public opinion. So I'm aware that a photo with gang symbols plays into one narrative of villainization, and I don't want to present a simplified narrative. I never want to oversimplify the complexities. The truth is gangs are here in George Floyd Square and they provide some protection, and gang members also do have conflict with people who step into their space. We should ask why. Why are there gangs? Who is affected? Sometimes divisions between rival gangs wind up fatal and that makes this painful. But here gangs are also included in this sacred space of our community. The creation of gangs is about exclusion. What does it mean to be excluded from society, and to create your own exclusive group that gives someone purpose? What protections do gangs offer their members that society doesn't, and why doesn't society offer that protection?

These are larger social questions we have to address. Part of the reason this country is where we are today, so fragmented, is because we don't ask why, don't connect the dots, and only go for the simplified narratives.

NOTES

1   This interview with Zalanga was conducted in early 2021.

2   On August 9, 2014, Michael Brown Jr., an unarmed Black man, was fatally shot by white police officer Darren Wilson in Ferguson, Missouri. The days and weeks after the killing were characterized by both peaceful and violent unrest in the city. On November 24, 2014, it was announced that a St. Louis County grand jury voted not to indict Officer Wilson for Brown's murder. Following the announcement, protests broke out in Ferguson and other US cities.

3   Major media outlets' initial coverage of the community's reaction to the grand jury announcement tended to focus on property destruction and violence. For example, see Monica Davey and Manny Fernandez, "Security in Ferguson is Tightened After Night of Unrest," *New York Times*, November 25, 2014, https://www.nytimes.com/2014/11/26/us/ferguson-missouri-violence.html, and Alan Taylor, "Violent Protests in Ferguson, Missouri," *The Atlantic*, November 25, 2014, https://www.theatlantic.com/photo/2014/11/violent-protests-in-ferguson-missouri/100860/. Later, commentary on the 2014 coverage appeared, with an attention to the relationship between police-sanctioned narratives, media organizations, social media, and activists on the ground. For example, see Jenée Desmond-Harris, "Twitter forced the world to pay attention to Ferguson. It won't last," *Vox*, January 14, 2015, https://www.vox.com/2015/1/14/7539649/ferguson-protests-twitter; Dominique Apollon et al, "Moving the Race Conversation Forward," Race Forward: The Center for Racial Justice Innovation (website), September 2014, http://act.colorlines.com/acton/attachment/1069/f-012e/1/-/-/-/-/Moving_Race_Conversation_Forward_Ferguson.pdf; and Byron B. Craig and Stephen E. Rahko, "Visual Profiling as Biopolitics: Or, Notes on Policing in Post-Racial #AmeriKKKa," *Cultural Studies ↔ Critical Methodologies* 2016, Vol 16(3) 287-295.

4   On March 7, 1965, nonviolent Civil Rights activists began a planned protest walk from Selma to Montgomery, Alabama. Though unarmed, the marchers were attacked by state troopers who wielded billy clubs and used tear gas. The event became dubbed "Bloody Sunday" and was one of the highly publicized and instrumental moments in ultimately securing the passage of the Voting Rights Act. On the fiftieth anniversary, in 2015, thousands gathered at the Selma bridge to commemorate the legacy of the 1960s Civil Rights activists and to issue renewed calls for equality. On November 15, 2015, Jamar Clark was shot by Minneapolis Police. He subsequently died. In response, protests and demonstrations occurred in Minneapolis over the next eighteen days. Neither officer involved in the shooting was charged. For more on the killing of George Floyd, see the Introduction of *Through the Lens*.

5   For more on the presence of white supremacists at the Minneapolis George Floyd protests, see, for example, Jaclyn Peiser, "'Umbrella Man' went viral breaking windows at a protest. He was a white supremacist trying to spark violence, police say," *Washington Post*, July 29, 2020, https://www.washingtonpost.com/nation/2020/07/29/umbrella-man-white-supremacist-minneapolis/, and for a focus on local responses to the potential presence of white supremacists, see Justin Glawe and Kate Briquelet, "Minneapolis Neighborhood Patrols Fear White Supremacists Are Infiltrating to Derail Protests," Daily Beast, June 5, 2020, https://www.thedailybeast.com/minneapolis-neighborhoods-fear-white-supremacists-are-infiltrating-to-derail-george-floyd-protests.

6   The question of whether to use the terms "looting" and "looter" has occurred at earlier moments, for instance with coverage of Hurricane Katrina, where the debate pitted "looting" against "finding" or "surviving." See, for example, Aaron Kinney, "'Looting' or 'Finding'?" Salon, September 2, 2005, http://www.salon.com/2005/09/02/photo_controversy/.

7   A November 2020 report by the Tishman Environment and Design Center at The New School states: "Hennepin Energy Resource Center, in downtown Minneapolis, is the largest MSW [municipal solid waste] incinerator in the state burning 1,200 tons of waste per day and is located beside North Minneapolis where many of the city's Black population has been segregated by decades of discriminatory policies." See the Tishman Environment and Design Center in consultation with GAIA and in collaboration with Moja Robinson, "The Cost of Burning Trash: Human and Ecological Impacts of Incineration in Minnesota," https://static1.squarespace.com/static/5d14dab43967cc000179f3d2/t/5fc653c09ee0f32b872b d1c4/1606833089063/Minnesota.pdf. The authors further note, "Evidence has linked an increased risk of death from COVID-19 to long-term exposure to particulate matter, a dangerous air pollutant, and that the risks from the virus are especially deadly for those living in communities with elevated levels of air pollution," such as those who live in proximity to incinerators. See the Tishman Environment and Design Center's "Projects and Publications" page, https://www.tishmancenter.org/projects-publications.

8   Chauvin, who was fired from the Minneapolis Police Department in the wake of George Floyd's killing, was ultimately convicted, in April 2021, of second-degree unintentional murder, third-degree murder, and second-degree manslaughter in the death of Floyd.

9   Breonna Taylor, a 26-year-old Black woman, was shot and killed by police in her Kentucky home on March 13, 2020, as three white officers attempted to force entry to her apartment during a raid that was based on faulty information. She had been in bed when the police arrived. Ultimately, none of the officers was charged in her death. This killing, along with other killings of Black individuals by police, led to numerous protests around the US throughout 2020.

10   Baldwin (1924–87) was an influential Black American writer and a spokesperson for civil rights.

11   This south Minneapolis gang, known as the Rolling (or Rollin) 30s Bloods, is often described in the news with regard to their violence. For instance, see Libor Jany and Liz Sawyer, "As Twin Cities street gangs evolve, traditional hierarchies vanish," *Star Tribune*, February 5, 2020, https://www.startribune.com/as-twin-cities-street-gangs-evolve-traditional-hierarchies-vanish/567512932/. Since Floyd's murder and the establishment of George Floyd Square, some journalists have reported on the presence of gang members at the Square, and the relationships between local activists, gangs, and police. See, for instance, Deena Winter, "Volunteers who help manage George Floyd Square work with the Bloods gang, but not police. Here's why," *Minnesota Reformer*, January 11, 2021, https://minnesotareformer.com/2021/01/11/volunteers-who-help-manage-george-floyd-square-work-with-the-bloods-gang-but-not-police-heres-why/.

4 SPENCER PLATT

SPENCER PLATT, *an American photojournalist on staff with the Getty Images wire service, has covered the Iraq War, the plight of displaced Congolese, the minority Kurds in Turkey, the conflict in the Central African Republic, fighting in Gaza, Syrians displaced by the country's ongoing civil war, the Peshmerga and refugees in Iraqi Kurdistan, and the recent war in Ukraine, among other places and peoples in crisis.*

Platt has won numerous honors for his work, including multiple awards from the Pictures of the Year International competition, the New York Press Photographers Association's Year In Pictures, and the National Press Photographers Association's Best of Photojournalism competition. In 2007, Platt received the World Press Photo of the Year award for an image taken in Beirut, Lebanon.

LAUREN WALSH / **What particular ethical issues have you encountered in covering Covid-19?[1]**

SPENCER PLATT / When you talk about any medically related story, any story with patients involved, then you definitely have to consider issues of privacy. I tried to get pictures inside hospitals, but they're controlling about letting media in; they're focused on patient privacy and that means it's that much harder to show the public what is happening—and yet this is something the public needs to take very seriously. How do you bridge that divide?

By mid-March and April in New York City, when it was the hot spot, the worst place in the world in terms of cases, some of the journalistic customs went by the wayside because it's just so imperative to capture the immediacy of the depth of the crisis. There were times I camped outside of a New York City hospital, trying to get an image that could convey the gravity of the situation. I wound up with pictures of people on stretchers, sometimes pictures of corpses, or I would be at funeral homes. They are not easy pictures to look at, but the threat this pandemic has posed outweighs an approach full of niceties.

I'll give an anecdote from photographing outside of hospitals. The ambulance drivers are generally friendly and outgoing; they understand the presence of media. They let us photograph what they're doing and when they bring patients out of the vehicle. But patients themselves aren't as receptive to the press. I get it; I don't know if I would want a camera documenting me if I were in that situation. I and most of my colleagues will respect patient privacy when we can, trying not to show someone's face, which isn't always easy. But one particular time I was outside a major hospital in a Hasidic neighborhood in Brooklyn that was, at that point, experiencing a huge surge in Covid cases. Again, the ambulance drivers were aware of me and working with me. But as an elderly man was brought out on a stretcher and saw me, he pulled his mask down, stared at me, and said, "Scum." A comment like that can make you go home at night and consider your profession: why am I doing this?

But I've been at this work a long time, and it didn't faze me. My job is to document, and at this moment, thousands of coronavirus patients were moving through that hospital. When the hospitals deny access to the press, then we have to find other ways to show the story. It's not that I'm not sensitive to the man who called me scum, but there was, then, a large contingent of Americans who thought this [pandemic] was a hoax or not that serious. I have to contribute documentation that shows what is going on here.

Here are two other examples [Figures 4.1 and 4.2]. I don't think either of these patients is aware of my presence. I try to be quick and discreet. These pictures are both taken from public property; I'm on a sidewalk. So, as a journalist, I had every right to take the photos, even every right to show their faces had I wanted to.

For the first image, I'm standing across the street from a hospital. I don't think you can recognize that individual. The second photo, also taken during the height of the crisis in New York City, is shot with a long lens, probably a 200 or 300 millimeter. It was taken outside of a residence; a lot of people died at home, not just in hospitals, and we need to show that as well. In general, with these kinds of photos from outside hospitals or homes, can you ever recognize the individual?

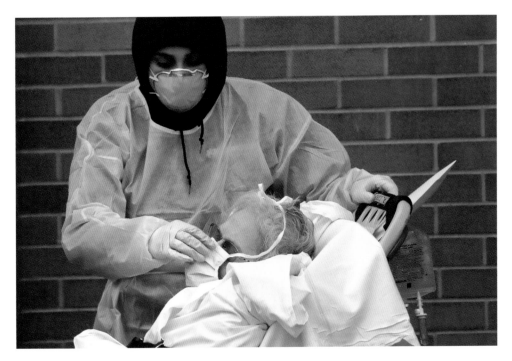

Figure 4.1 / Medical workers accept patients outside of a special coronavirus intake area at Maimonides Medical Center in the Borough Park neighborhood of Brooklyn. New York City, April 14, 2020.

Photo by Spencer Platt/Getty Images

Figure 4.2 / An individual, suspected to have coronavirus, is taken to an ambulance on April 11, 2020, in Brooklyn, New York.

Photo by Spencer Platt/Getty Images

Maybe at times. It's a fine line you have to walk, respecting someone's privacy and showing the story of a virus that is killing average people.

Think back to the recent US-Mexico border crisis and further back to the AIDS crisis of the 1980s. Look at photos from those situations, whether it be the migrant emergency or the earlier pandemic, that demonstrate that the pros of fully protecting individual privacy are superseded by the magnitude of the crisis.[2]

LW / When photographing in New York City, your hometown, as opposed to being in a foreign locale, do you have a greater awareness of trying to portray victims with dignity?

SP / The stock answer is absolutely no difference. But really I think it comes down to your subconscious, and this applies beyond one's hometown and includes one's whole country. For example, I was covering a hurricane a few years ago in Florida. The news media was focused on the upcoming destruction and devastation, and a lot of people fled to a sports stadium that was operating as a safe destination. I remember taking a photo of a woman who looked quite wealthy. She was crying. I felt somewhat uneasy about taking that photo. In hindsight, maybe it was because my in-laws live not very far away and this looked like someone they could have known.

Over my career, I've covered a lot of trauma, but often it was a plane ticket away. Maybe Haiti, or farther away, Iraq or Afghanistan. When you're covering disasters, it's often the lower middle class and the working class that are stuck in these refugee-like places; the middle class and upper middle class have the means to get out. This moment in Florida forced me to think about why I felt uncomfortable with the photo and about the kinds of photos we usually see when it comes to crisis and trauma, both abroad and here in America. I mean that there are preconceived ideas or even expectations of what the subject of a disaster photo looks like.

LW / Regarding Covid coverage specifically, were you thinking about any preconceived ideas in terms of the portrayal of subjects?

SP / Yes, I'll give you an example where I thought about whether my images would be seen as finger-pointing or shaming the subjects. In Brooklyn, there is one of the biggest Hasidic communities outside of Israel. I've covered this community many times, whether for holidays and festivals or for violence, or some other event. It can be a closed-off community, and in the early days of the pandemic there was a lot of press about this community's reluctance to abstain from mass gatherings, at funerals and that sort of thing.

As a photojournalist, I'm decidedly not there to shame this community. My images are not my attempt to editorialize. Personally, I have much respect for this community; they lead lives that are not addicted to technology like the rest of us. But on a purely scientific level, many were disregarding the city orders about public gatherings and recommendations to wear PPE.[3]

Here [Figure 4.3] you're looking at a funeral. Hundreds of people gathered for this ceremony. As you can see there are many individuals wearing masks, but not everyone. This community was

Figure 4.3 / Hundreds of members of the Orthodox Jewish community in Borough Park, Brooklyn attend a funeral for a rabbi who died from the coronavirus, April 5, 2020, New York City.

Photo by Spencer Platt/Getty Images

hit hard by the virus.[4] This funeral was for a rabbi, who had lost his life to complications arising from Covid.[5]

LW / Did you face particular health and safety risks in covering Covid?

SP / I remember in mid-March meeting up with a bunch of journalists over a bite to eat. We were talking about our photos and one said, nonchalantly, "I bet someone at this table has Covid." We didn't realize at the time, but that turned out to be true. So some of this "cavalier-ness" maybe is tied to being a journalist, where we often think we are immune—whether it's bullets in a war zone ("I'll never get hit!") or disease at home. I've been exposed to this way of thinking from the beginning of my career, but I believe some of us are slowly beginning to acknowledge the need to take this very seriously. I mean, before March, "PPE" wasn't even in the lexicon. So when we first started covering this, we didn't fully understand the risks that we, journalists, were facing. But after a time, I was certainly using face coverings, like a bandana, to protect myself.

LW / How has covering Covid or Black Lives Matter protests compared with covering conflict zones abroad?

SP / There are parallels, but differences too. First and foremost is the ease that you feel if you're covering right at home because you know the language and culture. So often I'm sent to a foreign place and I don't speak the language, don't truly understand the culture, how it ticks, and in those cases, you feel like an outsider. I mean, I love to work abroad, but there *is* a sense of relaxation when you're covering your country. And maybe that's a concern. Potentially, you can forget your journalistic status, your role as an inquiring observer, because this is your space, and you have family here and feelings connected to the issues you cover; you're more wrapped up in the story itself.

At the same time, covering domestically still involves getting to know the place. I was sent to Portland [Oregon] in July to cover the Black Lives Matter protests because they were ongoing and federal police were called in, and the nightly standoffs were quite intense: burning buildings, rubber bullets, and so on.[6] In this sense, my assignment in Portland wasn't so different from any other assignment with travel. It's normal as a wire photographer to jet into a place you don't know, whether it be Central African Republic or Portland, Oregon. Obviously, as an American photographer, I know Portland a little bit more. But the point is this is a city that has a huge history, and these protests have been going on, nightly, for a long time; there is so much nuanced tension there. All of a sudden you're sent in to document, and it takes some time to get a feel for how it works there.

LW / Was it dangerous?

SP / That's me on the left [Figure 4.4], wearing a helmet and gas mask, carrying my cameras. As you can see, there is tear gas that the federal police are spraying everywhere. For the most part, they were respectful to legitimate working press—myself with Getty, my colleagues from Reuters, AP, and other news outlets.

Figure 4.4 / A photographer, Platt, walks behind federal law enforcement officers as demonstrators protest against racial inequality and police violence in Portland, Oregon, July 26, 2020.

Photo by Caitlin Ochs/Reuters

There were dozens and dozens of protesters, people obviously part of the protest movement, that had "Press" written on their bike helmets or their jackets. These activists are mimicking press in order to protect themselves from police.[7] This was the first time I had seen that. It creates a gray zone. The police don't always know who is actual press or not. So there were a few times when cops ran up to me, with their gas masks on, and grabbed my press credentials, to verify who I am. Then they let me go on my way. There's an understanding of the role that the press plays in reporting events to the public.

The rise of this new gray zone matters because the term "press" used to be respected, at least it was in most contexts, as the person displaying a press card or a press decal was there purely as a neutral observer. Of course, many publications have political leanings, but in general, "press" meant that you were assigned to document an event and were not actively taking part in that event. With the explosion of online media sites and blogs, the stricter standards of past journalism are often jettisoned, and now anyone with a good printer is a "journalist." But blurring this line [between journalist and activist] puts the press at risk and undercuts the idea of neutral reportage. So please, don't call yourself a journalist for protection and then pick up a bottle and throw it—which I've witnessed.

At these Portland protests, I saw all walks of life: Army veterans, moms, really peaceful people. The majority were peaceful and respectful, but there was also some violence. Obviously, that means there could be risks to journalists' safety, but it's also important in terms of ethics: you

Figure 4.5 / Federal police clash with protesters in front of the Mark O. Hatfield federal courthouse in downtown Portland, as the city experiences a night of unrest. At this point, protesters had faced off in violent clashes with the Portland Police Bureau and federal police for over fifty-five straight nights. July 25, 2020.

Photo by Spencer Platt/Getty Images

have to be careful how you cover these situations. You need to visually portray the complexities. You need to be honest to what the situation is. If you just saw this photo [Figure 4.5], you would think this was a war zone.

So I ask myself: did I get an accurate portrayal? Because it's easy to just show the violence or chaos or tear gas, but that's not accurate to what happened, which was six hours of protests a day and maybe one or two hours were that chaotic. I think it's easier for a writer to put that into a paragraph than it is for a photographer to show it. And in the current media landscape I worry that the quieter images—from Portland or NYC or wherever [Figures 4.6 and 4.7]—don't have as much a chance to resonate. The media environment is too loud and too crowded.

But look, America in general is a visual country, open to images, and there is so much out there to document that is so important.

Figure 4.6 / People gather to protest in front of the Mark O. Hatfield federal courthouse as the city experiences another night of unrest, July 27, 2020, Portland, Oregon.

Photo by Spencer Platt/Getty Images

Figure 4.7 / Tape is placed over the mouths of figures adorning a historic building near where protesters affiliated with Black Lives Matter and other groups have congregated in a park outside City Hall in Lower Manhattan on June 30, 2020, in New York City.

Photo by Spencer Platt/Getty Images

NOTES

1   This interview with Platt was conducted in fall 2020.

2   In 2017–18, enormous caravans of migrants fled Central American countries for the United States, most trying to escape poverty, violence, or other threats. In April 2018, the Trump administration instituted a "zero tolerance" policy to deter illegal immigration that allowed, among other things, for parents to be separated from their children. Photographers documented these situations. For instance, an image by John Moore of Getty Images went viral in June of that year. The photo portrays a crying toddler next to her mother who is being searched by a border patrol officer. This family was not separated, but the picture of the child's tear-stained face became part of a political debate and a critique of family separation. Trump signed an executive order ending separations that same month following extensive public outcry, though the rest of the policy remained in effect. The Moore photo can be viewed at
    https://www.worldpressphoto.org/collection/photo/2019/37620/1/John-Moore. The AIDS crisis was at its height in the 1980s and 1990s in the US. To date, approximately 700,000 people have died of HIV/AIDS in the US. One of the most known American images of this crisis, a photo by Therese Frare, portrays 32-year-old David Kirby, whose dark eyes and emaciated face attest to the ravages of AIDS. The picture, taken on his deathbed, shows him surrounded by family, and can be viewed at
    https://www.life.com/history/behind-the-picture-the-photo-that-changed-the-face-of-aids/.

3   On March 15, the US Centers for Disease Control and Prevention (CDC) advised a halt to any gatherings of more than fifty people. Five days later, New York Governor Andrew Cuomo issued an order, "New York State on PAUSE," which canceled or postponed "non-essential gatherings…of any size for any reason," mandated six-foot social distancing requirements, limited outdoor recreational activities, and specified that any "concentration of individuals outside their home" was limited to "workers providing essential services." The City of New York closed bars, restaurants, and public schools on March 16 and 17. Cuomo officially required face masks in public on April 15. See Governor Cuomo's "New York State on PAUSE" executive order, which went into effect on March 22, https://www.governor.ny.gov/news/governor-cuomo-signs-new-york-state-pause-executive-order.

4   While no agencies track data strictly according to religious affiliation, data collected according to ZIP code indicated that by April, Borough Park and Greenpoint/Williamsburg (two Brooklyn neighborhoods with large Hasidic/Orthodox populations) were seeing excess at-home deaths at levels far above the city's average. In April, Hasidic news outlets were already estimating that hundreds of members of the Orthodox community in New York City had died. Beginning in March and at least through October 2020, Borough Park, Williamsburg, and Midwood, another Brooklyn neighborhood with a significant Hasidic population, were consistently reporting Covid positive test rates at levels higher than the city's average, with Borough Park, in particular, often reporting the highest levels in Brooklyn.

5   New York City police broke up this funeral because gatherers congregated in violation of the city's social distancing rules.

6   Beginning in May 2020, in reaction to the killing of George Floyd, Portland, Oregon, was the site of repeated protests, including heated standoffs between civilians and law enforcement. The protests continued for months. In July, federal forces were deployed to protect a US courthouse, which had been vandalized. Throughout the protests, other federal buildings, US courthouses, and an ICE facility were also damaged. See, for example, Tom Batchelor, "Portland Protesters Have Caused $2.3 Million in Damage to Federal Buildings," *Newsweek*, February 4, 2021, https://www.newsweek.com/portland-protesters-damage-cost-federal-buildings-1566821.

7   Portland city officials said that federal agents exceeded their authority to control protesters and, in cases, seriously injured some of the peaceful activists. See, for example, Kate Conger and Nicholas Bogel-Burroughs, "Fact Check: How Violent Are the Portland Protests?" *New York Times*, July 28, 2020, https://www.nytimes.com/2020/07/28/us/portland-protests-fact-check.html. At times, local police also used force against protesters, even before the arrival of federal agents in July. For a description of their tactics and examples of protesters' injuries, see, for instance, "Shot in the Head," Physicians for Human Rights

(website), September 14, 2020,
https://storymaps.arcgis.com/stories/29cbf2e87b914dbaabdec2f3d350839e, and Alice Speri,
"Portland Reckons with Police Attacks on Protesters after Months of Unrest,"
The Intercept, October 25, 2020, https://theintercept.com/2020/10/25/portland-reckons-with-police-violence-on-protesters-after-months-of-unrest/. Portland also witnessed aggressive tactics from police towards the media specifically. For more on this, see, for instance, Rachel Treisman, "Order Temporarily Blocks Feds From Targeting Press And Legal Observers In Portland," NPR, July 23, 2020,
https://www.npr.org/sections/live-updates-protests-for-racial-justice/2020/07/23/894953202/order-temporarily-blocks-feds-from-targeting-press-and-legal-observers-in-portla, as well as note 40 in the Introduction to Through the Lens.

INTERVIEWS WITH

PHOTOJOURNALISTS OUTSIDE THE US

5 RODRIGO ABD

RODRIGO ABD *is a staff photographer with the Associated Press (AP). Born in Argentina, he is currently based in Peru. He has covered upheaval in Bolivia, gang violence in Guatemala, natural disaster in Haiti, conflict in Libya and Syria, and he has embedded twice with US troops in Afghanistan.*

In 2013, he was part of the AP team that won the Pulitzer Prize for Breaking News Photography for coverage of the civil war in Syria. He has won the Maria Moors Cabot Prize from Columbia University for excellence in coverage of Latin America and the Caribbean, as well as awards from World Press Photo, Pictures of the Year International, the Overseas Press Club of America, and the China International Press Photo Contest, among others.

LAUREN WALSH   /   With some of your Covid-19 coverage, it's obvious that you're very close to medical workers or patients. What kind of safety precautions are you taking?[1]

RODRIGO ABD   /   I looked to how the European photographers were protecting themselves in March when Covid surged there, when it was only just starting here.[2] I was watching this and thinking, "How are the European or the American photographers protecting themselves?" I tried to copy the strategies I saw them using.

But the problem was, in the first weeks here, it was very difficult to find PPE—the good masks, the suits. I have gas masks that I use in conflict and in riots, but here [Lima, Peru] it was summertime and it's very hard to wear that heavy gear. Plus, it's one thing to wear the PPE when you're working in a hospital; people see that as normal for that setting. But I can't dress in a full-body suit in the streets. I want to get close to people, and you can't achieve that if you look like an astronaut in the middle of the city. That becomes a barrier between myself as photographer and the people I hope to document. So I wanted to protect myself, but, by and large, I used protective gear that was less imposing-looking than the full suits. I had a mask and had sanitizer with me at all times.

At the end of the day, I had to be very careful in transitioning from work to home. I live with my wife and daughter, and don't want them sick. So I turned my car into a "bunker." All clothes from the day came off there, my cameras stayed there. I wiped down everything with alcohol. I would just bring the memory card inside the house because I didn't want my computer in the car with the exposed items.

LW   /   In your coverage of Covid and its impact, were you ever denied access by hospitals or government authorities?

RA   /   Yes, at different times. Early on, journalists were allowed in the hospitals, but after April, the hospitals started collapsing; they couldn't handle the numbers of patients. Then it was really difficult to get inside. So I tried to cover the story in a different way, working with funeral homes, and with private workers that were contracted by the state to pick up bodies all over the city.

When the situation started getting better a bit in September and October, then it was easier to get back inside the hospitals. And compared to other countries, for instance in Europe, I think we had decent access. But, you know, the authorities weren't telling the public how bad the situation is, that the hospitals are completely overburdened. Officials tried to hide that as much as possible when it was really bad here.

LW / You mean the Peruvian government was concealing or misrepresenting information about the extent of the Covid crisis?

RA   /   I don't know official numbers, but organizations said the death rate this year was almost double what the government was reporting. But I think that was happening all around the world. For the journalists here, it was easy to see that the government's numbers were false. For example, they announce "100 people died yesterday" and I know the true number is higher because I'm with the private workers who are collecting the dead, and we see thirty deaths in just one

Figure 5.1 / Gladys Ramos sits next to the tomb of her uncle Saturnino Zumia, who died of Covid-19, in Comas, on the outskirts of Lima, Peru, July 21, 2020. At this time, the Pan American Health Organization and other agencies were investigating whether the country failed to classify over 27,000 deaths as caused by coronavirus, a figure that could have more than doubled the country's official death toll from the disease.

Photo by Rodrigo Abd/AP

sector of Lima, while people are dying all over the city and the country, and communities in the jungle were getting hit really hard just then. So the number had to be higher than the 100 the government was reporting. Maybe it was a strategy of the government to keep people from being alarmed.

LW / So the government is potentially under-reporting the death toll. Can your images help to counter that?

RA / Well, some of my pictures are published here in Peru, but not many. Most of my pictures wind up published internationally. It is probably the case that local outlets want to give priority to their own photographers instead of purchasing from the AP. But I think the local newspapers were also trying to be very cautious in the first months of coverage and careful about publishing reports that differed from what the government was telling the public. There was one news-paper that did speak up, but it's an underground, leftist paper.[3] Otherwise, the biggest newspapers and the TV stations were very cautious on that; they reported the number that the government cited. So they were not really reporting just how hard the situation was for families and for people on the streets, or the indigenous people who live in the jungle.

I think one thing that happened was that news outlets started seeing our work on the [AP] wire. And then they also started doing more reporting about the reality, the accuracy, of what was really happening in Peru. For example, we did a story about a group of people working for a funeral home. They're migrants from Venezuela, many of them illegal, and they were doing the job of picking up all these bodies all over the city for fifteen hours a day.[4] The local newspapers and TV saw our coverage, and those outlets started reporting those stories as well, because they were interesting and they were more accurately reflecting the actuality of suffering at the time.

In Peru, we have a bad economic situation, and regional media organizations can depend on official, state money as well as private sources.[5] But if you report "badly," for example on the government, there may be pushback, financial or otherwise.[6]

Some of the newspapers and TV programs were trying [early on] to be quiet about the reality of the Covid situation. They were trying to do some stories on the crisis, but they weren't showing that the country was immersed in death. It's a terrible situation for the local news to be so dependent on powerful stakeholders for funds or approval. This is why, I think, it is not common to see an investigative story about our government. The news media have to be very cautious.[7]

LW / You have had plenty of experience covering war and gang violence. Does covering Covid feel similar?

RA / It is similar in the way that you need to immerse yourself in the reality of those who are living with the crisis. You've got to get to the heart of the story. It's that idea that you have to wake up every single day, and every single day, you have to go and comprehensively cover that story.

We have to document really well, have to work really hard, despite the risks. But what is different from covering traditional conflict is now I am covering the conflict and facing the risk in the same city where I live with my family. That makes a difference.

It's not the same as going back to a hotel at the end of a day, having some food and editing your photos.[8] Now I go back to a small apartment. I need to play with my daughter and help with cooking and with laundry. The isolation has been so hard on everyone, so I *need* to be there. But basically, it's exhausting.

Another difference, for example, you go cover Afghanistan with a military battalion, you know that you are going to cover a specific story. You go to Libya and you know Gaddafi is the story. He is either going to leave the country or be killed, or there will be a military coup.[9] The problem with *this* coverage is there is no end, or at least no end that is coming soon. You never see the end and psychologically that's complex and heavy.

And the "conflict" is at home. You're covering dying, death, funerals, grief—all right at home. Sometimes with funerals, people celebrate the dead, they drink together; other times at these funeral homes, everyone is crying, they're breaking down. You're trying to absorb all of it and trying to document carefully what you see. So you push your emotions aside, but you're taking all of those emotions in. So then you put those emotions in a bag, and you carry that bag. Sometimes it is nice to carry that bag; you can deal with it. And sometimes it's really hard; it's very difficult to sleep, to get away from those emotions.

LW / Here is one case where you were very close both to someone's death and to the family member who survived him. Tell me about this photo [Figure 5.2].

RA / The story was that the hospitals were so collapsed that people never made it to them. They'd call for help and medical services would never show up. So the sick were just dying in their homes. This was in May and June.

I was focusing on families in poorer neighborhoods. I was trying to show their story, their daily life, their homes, their tables, their chairs, their dogs and cats. I wanted to show where they were dying, and also where they lived before they died. I wanted to show if they died sleeping or waiting for help.

For this photo, the daughter of Ricardo Noriega spoke to us. She was waiting for us when we arrived. She said that he died on the sofa, the same sofa that he has had for years. The framing here is very important for showing that.[10]

At that moment, it was a new thing to grasp that people were dying in their houses, because nobody was reporting that story. But there were no more beds in any hospitals. So you'd hear: "You have the symptoms? I am sorry, wait in your house to die." *That* was a story that we wanted to tell.

LW / That photo personalizes one single death, whereas this one [Figure 5.3] conveys the vastness of death.

Figure 5.2 / Ricardo Noriega, seventy-seven, lies dead on the floor of his living room. He died with great difficulty in breathing, one of the most characteristic symptoms of Covid-19. Lima, Peru, May 4, 2020.

Photo by Rodrigo Abd/AP

Figure 5.3 / During the Corpus Christi mass in Lima's main cathedral, Archbishop Carlos Castillo swings a censer, spreading incense before more than 5,000 portraits of people who died from Covid-19, Peru, June 14, 2020. At this time, more than 225,000 had been infected in the country.

Photo by Rodrigo Abd/AP

RA /   This is in the main Peruvian cathedral. There is the archbishop of the diocese of Lima, throwing incense, and he will be giving a mass that will be broadcast on TV. The day before that mass, the workers of the church put up all these portraits that relatives sent in. They printed the images right there at the church. For me, this was an amazing story. The people, the relatives, want others to see what is happening. This was a signal from the people. Everyone knows that this mass will be broadcast to millions of Peruvians. The people who suffered were not being represented in local media or by the government, and this was a way for them to gain voice. Collectively, they shout, "Look, this is massive. This is not only my relative. Look how many people are here on the benches and walls of this church." They were showing the rest of the country that didn't have an understanding of what was going on.

I lived in Guatemala for many years, and covered civil war there. When I saw these photos in the cathedral, I related them to the portraits of people who "disappeared" in the 1980s.[11] The military dictatorships were denying what was going on with the thousands of people that vanished, but the widows and mothers were in the streets, holding photos, reclaiming their dead loved ones. I felt a resonance with that and wanted to convey that here. This situation, like those of the disappeared who had no voice and no agency, is political. This is happening to so many people and they need help. When there is injustice occurring, people want others to know what is going on.

LW /   What do you mean it's political?

RA /   So many people have died here. The government was too late with its response. It could have been handled better and earlier.[12] This is an enormous trauma.

LW /   What is the story in terms of Covid and the indigenous population, especially those based in jungle areas of Peru?

RA /   In our country, the indigenous population is more or less a "forgotten population." They're more isolated. They're poor. The local governments have fewer resources. So the situation was really dramatic, really awful there.

It was difficult for me to move around. There are many villages and the only way between them is by boat, so I wasn't able to document all that they suffered. [See Figure 5.4]

They don't have even local doctors. Because of this, the Shipibo Indians of the central jungle of Peru decided to organize themselves, with their own resources, to save lives. They formed a group called "Comando Matico" in May with the goal of curing Covid-19 with medicinal jungle plants, such as matico, and traditional curatives like massages.[13] [See Figure 5.5]

Despite this community help and these ancestral treatments, many people continued to die in the jungle. One night, I accompanied a family in a canoe. We traveled for five hours, to an indigenous village, to be able to watch over their loved one who had died of the virus hours earlier.

Figure 5.4 / Passengers arrive in a public taxi boat to the Shipibo Indigenous community of Pucallpa, located along the Ucayali River in the Amazonian rainforest of eastern Peru, September 3, 2020, amid the coronavirus pandemic. Transportation is one of the biggest hurdles in treating indigenous groups, some of which can only be reached by an eight-hour boat ride.

Photo by Rodrigo Abd/AP

Figure 5.5 / Mery Fasabi, left, and Isai Eliaquin Sanancino carry a pot of herbs steeped in boiling water to the home of a woman infected with coronavirus, in the Shipibo Indigenous community of Pucallpa, in Peru's Ucayali region, September 1, 2020. Fasabi, along with fifteen other volunteers, has set up a makeshift treatment center, known locally as Comando Matico, that takes a holistic approach to treating the virus.

Photo by Rodrigo Abd/AP

The idea with this body of photography was to show what this indigenous population was facing, and when I was there, I realized just how dire it was because they were also battling dengue.[14] Yet they had no resources to deal with all this sickness.

It was hard, personally, to witness their conditions. The lack of infrastructure and the structural poverty is enormous. This is a vulnerable population that needs better help.

Figure 5.6 / Family members weep during the burial of Manuela Chavez, who died from symptoms related to the coronavirus at the age of eighty-eight, in the Shipibo Indigenous community of Pucallpa, in Peru's Ucayali region, August 31, 2020.

Photo by Rodrigo Abd/AP

LW / In the US, there is plenty of coverage of Covid, but we don't often see dead bodies. Sometimes this is due to privacy restrictions. But critics have noted that coverage from other parts of the world, for instance Peru and other countries in South America, is more graphic in this sense. Do you think that kind of explicit imagery is important?

RA / I think it's more accurate for what the story is. Over one million people [globally] have died. In terms of journalism, you have to highlight many parts of the story, and an integral component is the deaths. As a photojournalist, therefore, you have to show that. If you show how hard it is, how severe this crisis has become, and if you do so with respect and intelligence, you can make some people more sensitive to the situation and more alert toward the government's responsibility and their lack of proper action.

You *do* need to be considerate of people, especially victims and their loved ones, and you do need to get proper permission, for example, if you're inside a family's home. Of course, I did that with the family of Ricardo Noriega [Figure 5.2]. But you need to show exactly what is going on. It's the only way to document the truth of the story.[15] If you are not doing that, if you are censoring the story, it's like you are making it up; it's not the true or full story. That is not what we should do. We are journalists.

Many journalists did amazing stories about the courage of the doctors risking their lives, and the people working in the ambulances, and about volunteers collecting clothes and food to help others. These stories must be done, too. You have to show all aspects of this historic moment. It's our responsibility as documentarians.

NOTES

1   This interview with Abd was conducted in fall 2020.

2   For an example of early European coverage, see, for instance, photographer Fabio Bucciarelli's work in Bergamo, Italy: Jason Horowitz (Writer) and Fabio Bucciarelli (Photographs), "'We Take the Dead From Morning Till Night,'" *New York Times*, March 27, 2020,
https://www.nytimes.com/interactive/2020/03/27/world/europe/coronavirus-italy-bergamo.html.
For Bucciarelli's discussion of his safety precautions, see this webinar with Zoe Flood from the Frontline Freelance Register on April 1, 2020: https://www.facebook.com/watch/?v=146992473374848.

3   Abd is referring to the publication *Hildebrandt en sus trece*.

4   See the story: Franklin Briceño and Rodrigo Abd, "As virus swamps Peru, Venezuelan migrants collect the dead," AP News, May 21, 2020, https://apnews.com/article/c8988768299f792ffab2c8fa8409d0a3.

5   For more on this, see, for instance, Úrsula Freundt-Thurne, César Pita, and María José Ampuero, "Mapping Digital Media: Peru," Open Society Foundations (website), November 2012,
https://www.opensocietyfoundations.org/uploads/366253a3-774e-42af-b7b6-451651df28ec/mapping-digital-media-peru-20121112.pdf. See also Reporters Without Borders: Peru (website), as of July 1, 2021,
https://rsf.org/en/peru, as well as the infographic on political risks to Peru's media pluralism in Reporters Without Border's Media Ownership Monitor (website), as of July 2, 2021,
https://www.mom-rsf.org/en/countries/peru/.

6   Media watchdogs commonly cite forms of retribution against Peruvian journalists when covering "sensitive" topics. Of particular concern in Peru is that journalists can face reprisals, intimidation, and potential prosecution under the country's defamation laws. Critics further note that media organizations can lose private funding, particularly from advertisers, if the funder or stakeholder is displeased with the news content.

7   Pressure on media can disproportionately influence the coverage of local or regional media. See again the sources in note 5.

8 Abd uses "edit," as is common in the industry, to mean "select" or "choose," and potentially to apply minimal post-production techniques as allowed by the Associated Press.

9 The First Libyan Civil War (February–October 2011) was fought between forces loyal to Libyan leader Muammar Gaddafi and anti-Gaddafi rebels. In 2011, Gaddafi's government fell and he was captured and killed.

10 Abd adds, "I'm not sure if she was the one who ultimately moved his body to the floor, but I believe so; I think she had hoped she could help him breathe. But he was already dead."

11 During the civil war in Guatemala (1960–96) an estimated 200,000 people died. This number includes approximately 40,000 people who "disappeared" (*los desaparecidos*), in many cases likely the result of executions by government forces.

12 The Peruvian government did call for a lockdown beginning on March 16, when only seventy-one cases had been reported, and before countries like Brazil or the United Kingdom. The policy failures that nevertheless resulted in a disastrous outbreak have been written about, for example, in Teresa Welsh, "Inequality and corruption: Why Peru is losing its Covid-19 battle," Devex (website), July 1, 2020, https://www.devex.com/news/inequality-and-corruption-why-peru-is-losing-its-covid-19-battle-97604.

13 Matico is a flowering plant with a peppery odor and is native to the Caribbean and much of tropical America. It is used as an antiseptic by those who practice traditional, plant-based medicine.

14 Dengue, a mosquito-borne tropical disease, is characterized by fever, fatigue, vomiting, joint and muscle pain, and/or rash.

15 Abd's own coverage of the pandemic involves, at times, more explicit images, including the pictures of dead bodies. See, for instance, Briceño and Abd in note 4, above.

6   ALY SONG

ALY SONG is a staff photographer with Reuters. Born in western China, he is now based in Shanghai and covers primarily politics, culture, and economics in China. Prior to his work with Reuters, he was a photographer with a local Chinese newspaper.

In 2020, Song was nominated for the Reuters Journalists of the Year Awards and he won second place in the international Chromatic Awards photojournalism category. That same year, he also received an honorable mention from the Annual Photography Awards for photojournalism.

LAUREN WALSH / Were you the only Reuters photographer in Wuhan in the early days of the pandemic?[1]

ALY SONG / In the beginning of the Wuhan shutdown in late January, Reuters sent a couple of photojournalists to cover the story. But that's when they were first locking down the city and no one could guarantee the safety, or even accommodations, for these photojournalists, so they got on a train and they left for a neighboring province called Jiangxi. They covered the impact of the virus from there.

As for myself, on March 25, I arrived in Hubei Province [where Wuhan is located]. First, I went to the neighboring, smaller cities around Wuhan. And finally on March 27, I entered Wuhan and started covering the virus there.

LW / By the time you arrived, did you feel safe covering this, or were you unsure of how to work safely?

AS / I've had hostile environment training with Reuters, so I felt I knew how to protect myself, whether it's from the virus or other hostile circumstances.[2] And by the time I got to Wuhan, the Covid numbers weren't very high there. They had been in the thousands in January, but had dropped radically by March because the city had been in lockdown.[3] So even if the official numbers were under-reporting the actuality, I still felt safe enough to work there.

Figure 6.1 / Volunteers disinfect the Qintai Grand Theater in Wuhan, the Chinese epicenter of the outbreak, April 2, 2020.

Photo by Aly Song/Reuters

LW / What kinds of safety precautions did you take?

AS / I was working with a videographer and a reporter [from Reuters], and we operated as a team, having meetings and discussing safety and making decisions together. In addition, I was checking in frequently with editors. My location was known at all times. That's how we conducted our work in Wuhan.

Of course, I was also wearing PPE and I used alcohol to wipe down my camera gear. So for instance, for this photo [Figure 6.1], I am dressed just as those figures are. The only difference is that they're carrying sanitization equipment and I am carrying camera gear.

It was difficult to take this picture, or rather, I was nervous because I just didn't know if breathing in those fumes was safe. I'm glad I was wearing all the protective equipment.

LW / What was the mood like in Wuhan when you arrived?

AS / At the end of March, there still weren't many people out, walking around the streets. But the people you did encounter seemed "beat up," like they'd suffered a lot. And if you talked about the virus with them, 80% to 90% of them would start crying or otherwise get incredibly emotional about it. [See Figure 6.2] They were still very scared of the idea of the virus, but they were not scared of the camera, or of being documented.

This photo [Figure 6.3] shows how the presence of the virus became part of everyday life. This man is wearing full-body PPE and eating breakfast, a local noodle; it's a delicacy here. This is how people dressed for routine things, like grocery shopping. It gives you a sense of how life moved forward in a culture of fear.

LW / The previous example shows how cultural behaviors may adapt and move on. What does this next photo reveal? [See Figure 6.4]

AS / In a lot of cities in China, people live in residential neighborhoods that are gated. During the lockdown, yellow blockades, like the ones you see here, were placed at the entrance gates, to stop people from going in and out. There would be one or two policemen keeping watch. But people, like the woman in this photo, at times might find a "break" in the wall in order to go out shopping or for something else. I wanted to show the reality of the lockdown for the people of Wuhan. I wanted to show just how tough it was.

LW / Did you have hospital access in Wuhan?

AS / It's not easy to work inside a hospital, especially around patients with Covid. But we [Song and his two Reuters colleagues] did get into one place, a quarantine facility, even though the Covid numbers were down, so it was not as much of a story. We had connections in the facility and got access into the "red zone," which is where the active positive patients are. I was dressed in two layers of PPE, and the facility strictly controlled who went in and out.

Figure 6.2 / Dai Jinfeng cries while talking about not being able to see her mother due to quarantine restrictions, Wuhan, China, March 31, 2020.

Photo by Aly Song/Reuters

Figure 6.3 / A man wearing a protective suit eats his breakfast of Regan Noodles, a signature Wuhan dish of hot dried noodles, on a street in Wuhan, China, during the Covid-19 lockdown, April 2, 2020.

Photo by Aly Song/Reuters

Figure 6.4 / A woman wearing a face mask slips through barriers that have been set up to block off buildings and their residents, Wuhan, China, March 29, 2020.

Photo by Aly Song/Reuters

After photographing, my camera needed to be cleaned with UV light, to disinfect it. By then, I guess, word that journalists were in the Covid facility got out to local law enforcement, and a couple police cars plus twenty policemen and some politicians showed up at the facility. They tried to coerce me into deleting my photos.

For ten hours, we were in a doctor's office in the Covid facility arguing with local law enforcement. They told me and my colleagues that we weren't safe, in terms of the virus, because we had entered the facility. They implied we might be compelled to quarantine for two weeks. They were being very aggressive. They were using tactics to intimidate us and leverage us into destroying the documentation we had made. We tried reaching out to government officials to preserve the photos, but they couldn't do anything to help.

This all happened on April 7 and the reopening of Wuhan, the lifting of the lockdown, was coming up on the 8th. So we fought to keep this imagery, but we didn't want to lose the opportunity to work on the 8th, and if we'd kept arguing, that likely would have happened. That's what they were implying. In the end, we decided to focus on the upcoming events, and on the work we needed to do on the 8th. So the images were lost; the police formatted my SD card. The photos were wiped.

LW / Wuhan was doing well in terms of getting Covid cases under control. So why didn't the police want your photos to be public?

AS / That's a great question. To answer that, I have to explain a bit how Chinese society works. The photos themselves were *not* the problem. It was the fact that they existed at all. The question was: how did these reporters get into a Covid facility, into such a restricted area? The fact that we did, reflects badly not directly on the police but on the local politicians [who had not authorized this access, as the journalists obtained entry via connections with facility staff], and this becomes a concern for them if it holds them back from a promotion.

Journalism can be difficult in China, as in other places around the world. It's not that the people of China are hostile to journalists, but the government does monitor. There were times in Wuhan when I think I was surveilled. It makes it more difficult to work.

LW / Are there ever times when the government *helps* with gaining access?

AS / In a sense, yes. This photo [Figure 6.5], from April 8, the first day of the reopening of Wuhan, was at the Tianhe Airport. This was part of a government-sponsored propaganda trip, and here we're seeing medical personnel saying goodbye to each other. This specific group was from Manchuria, in northeast China, and they had been working together for over two months. It was like they had fought a war together.

Because this was a propaganda tour, flags were being flown, songs were being sung. It was meant to show to the people of the world a sense of great success. I'm personally not really interested in the propaganda side, but I was happy to be there, and happy that I was able to capture something real. The emotions you see in this image are real; they are not choreographed.

Figure 6.5 / Medical workers hug at the Wuhan Tianhe Airport before leaving for home after Wuhan's lockdown ended and travel restrictions were lifted, April 8, 2020.

Photo by Aly Song/Reuters

These orchestrated media tours are a fixture of Chinese society, and just because it is propaganda doesn't mean it's always a bad thing. The good parts are that you get access to places or scenes. For instance, if this particular tour hadn't happened, I may not have been able to get this photo of the medical personnel hugging. And in the end, I'm a journalist, so no matter what the circumstances, I will remain impartial in my documentation. It's then up to the consumer of these images to ask what is propaganda and what isn't. Viewers have to shape their own informed opinions.

Here is another example [Figure 6.6] from a different organized media tour after the lockdown had ended and children had returned to school. Aspects are artificial. In this case, it was almost funny how ridiculously talented each of these children was. It was as if they had been hand-picked because they sang perfectly, did beautiful calligraphy, played piano, and so on. So it's a set-up photo opportunity; but even so, you can see aspects of the education system at work. You see that they wear little red ties; you see how they're seated. Those are truths that show us how education is conducted.

Figure 6.6 / Students of the Changchun Street Primary School in Wuhan, China, September 4, 2020.

Photo by Aly Song/Reuters

LW / Are there aspects of the pandemic that you wanted to document but couldn't?

AS / It was an exhausting year and there were definitely things I wanted to document but didn't. One passion project was focused on animals used in scientific research, but the topic became increasingly sensitive during the pandemic, because animals were the source of the virus.[4] So I couldn't find anyone who agreed to be interviewed or documented on this. Another case was about a middle-aged couple in Wuhan. Each person had lost their respective husband or wife to Covid and then they met and formed a new family. It's a great story, but the children of this couple were not happy about the new family and didn't want this story told. As a journalist, I'm respectful when subjects don't want to be photographed, and I just have to continue to find or move on to new stories.

LW / You said it was an exhausting year. Tell me more about that.

AS / 2020 was the most professionally grueling and difficult year I have ever experienced. I remember working in late January. It was the time of the Spring Festival [Chinese Lunar New Year] and a time that you would spend with family.[5] But no one could celebrate because of the virus, and since I couldn't use this personal time, it was put toward work. From there, the virus just got worse and worse. The whole year, I felt like I was dragged by my nose.

Throughout 2020, I made four separate trips to Wuhan. The first time was three weeks in duration. The second time I was there one week. The third time was three days and the fourth time was two weeks. Added together, I spent about seven weeks documenting there. But the story was everywhere; there was no break from it. It wasn't just Wuhan.

LW / Thankfully, there has been a shift in China. What do you hope that a viewer thinks or feels in response to this image? [See Figure 6.7]

AS / There are two things about this photo. First, I felt it was unbelievable that this was taken less than one year after the start of the pandemic, and that people were already back to partying, to dancing around, like nothing had ever happened. Second, I hope this can encourage other countries that are still suffering from Covid by showing that this type of freedom and this type of celebration is around the corner. The suffering is temporary.

LW / Do you think that the public in China was given a good understanding of the crisis there, especially in the first few months of the pandemic?

AS / Chinese citizens are always very obedient when it comes to what the government tells them. They listen to what authorities say, and they do exactly what they're told. If they're told the sun is round, the sun is round. If they're told the sun is square, the sun is square.

The first couple months of the pandemic were very chaotic for people in China. But when the public was told they needed to be in lockdown, everybody fell into line. Because of this obedience, the problem was solved more easily, compared with other countries.

As for specific information from the government, what you see on the news is what officials *want* you to see. It's not necessarily the truth. Things are filtered. But as a journalist I endeavor to document the truth.

Figure 6.7 / People dance at a nightclub in Wuhan, China, almost a year after the global outbreak of Covid-19, December 12, 2020.

Photo by Aly Song/Reuters

LW / Having covered the pandemic, what insights do you now have?

Figure 6.8 / Dogs wear masks at a main shopping area, during the Covid-19 pandemic, in downtown Shanghai, China, February 16, 2020.

Photo by Aly Song/Reuters

AS / We are easily scared. Look at this photo [Figure 6.8], which was taken in Shanghai, when news came out that dogs could get Covid as well.[6] People started dressing their dogs in PPE out of fear.

This virus let us know that even though we have rockets, nuclear weapons, Teslas and Facebook—as much as these technological advances are forms of progress—we are still very behind as a species. We have so much to learn.

NOTES

1   This interview with Song was conducted in early 2021.

2   For more on hostile environment training, see note 7 in the Kenon interview.

3   When Wuhan went under lockdown in late January, the city was recording a seven-day average of over 400 new cases per day. By March 27, when Song arrived, there had only been two cases in the past ten days. See Lauren Gardner, "Mapping Covid-19," Johns Hopkins University Center for Systems Science and Engineering Covid-19 Project (website), January 23, 2020, https://systems.jhu.edu/research/public-health/ncov/.

4   The virus that causes Covid-19, also known as SARS-CoV-2, is believed to have originated in bats, although how the transmission from animal to human occurred, with this particular virus, has not been confirmed.

5   Lunar New Year (also known as Chinese New Year and Spring Festival) is a celebration of the new year according to the traditional Chinese lunisolar calendar.

6   There is no evidence that dogs play any significant role in the transmission of the coronavirus, though there have been limited documented cases of dogs becoming infected with Covid, generally after close contact with a person who has Covid.

INTERVIEWS WITH

DIRECTORS OF PHOTOGRAPHY

7 DANESE KENON

DANESE KENON *is the Director of Video and Photography at the* Philadelphia Inquirer. *She was a visual fellow at the Poynter Institute, holds a master's degree in photography from the S.I. Newhouse School of Public Communications at Syracuse University, and won a Pulliam Fellowship with the* Indianapolis Star. *She has worked as a visuals editor at the* Pittsburgh Post-Gazette *and was later the Deputy Director of Video/Multimedia at the* Tampa Bay Times.

Kenon teaches leadership and multimedia journalism at the Kalish Workshop, based at Rochester Institute of Technology, and through the National Press Photographers Association (NPPA), in addition to working with students in the National Association of Black Journalists. She is part of the 2021 NPPA's Best of Photojournalism executive team.

LAUREN WALSH / You have a staff of thirteen photographers. Do they have freedom to generate their own story ideas and if so, were any such enterprise pieces focused on Covid?[1]

DANESE KENON / It was difficult for photographers to pitch enterprise work in 2020 because the year was just so unpredictable. Even so, our photographers came up with good ideas. For instance, Jessica Griffin pitched an idea to embed with an ambulance company, early in the pandemic.[2] That wound up being our first really close-up look at Covid in Philadelphia. She showed what it was like in terms of treating patients, seeing their suffering and frailty, seeing them in their home, and she captured the stress and exhaustion of the medical workers as well as their compassion.

At the same time, once Jessica was on this, we had to pull her off the street. Because this story placed her so near to people with Covid, there was a real exposure risk, and we took that very seriously. So even if the photographer tests negative, after exposure we did not want them in close proximity to other people. They could work outdoors through their fourteen-day [quarantine] period—exteriors of buildings, shots like that.[3] But we didn't want to endanger Philadelphians. There was a lot of testing and a lot of waiting, even with negative tests, through these periods.

LW / Did you have photographers inside hospitals as well?

DK / We had a photographer-videographer combo inside Temple University Hospital [in Philadelphia] as early as April. The hospital gave access, but there were a lot of restrictions on our journalists.

Of course, I was worrying about journalist safety. For instance, whatever protection the doctors were wearing, I wanted our journalists to have, too. But I also didn't want to take critical PPE from the hospital. We need to cover what's happening, but we don't want to be a part of the problem. So this coverage raised new challenges. You're thinking about safety from everyone's perspective and you're also thinking about privacy, because we couldn't violate HIPAA [Health Insurance Portability and Accountability Act], which meant in practice that we could not publish photos that revealed who a patient is. We have images of doctors, of nurses, but you'll notice that the photos with patients are careful to protect their identity.[4] [See an example, Figure 7.1]

It's been nearly a year since the shutdown began in March, and our recent [January 2021] hospital coverage feels different. It used to be that our photographer had to dress up in PPE like a space alien and the stress was everywhere. Now it's still very critical, but there has been some relief as we understand this disease better.

We also have more access with patients. We can talk with the patients, and get their permission to photograph their faces or document their experiences. Jessica Griffin was able to capture more intimate situations, such as an emergency room nurse giving medicine to a patient, a couple waiting for an IV infusion, and a nurse cleaning up the aftermath inside a trauma room. This was noticeably different from the access that was previously granted.[5]

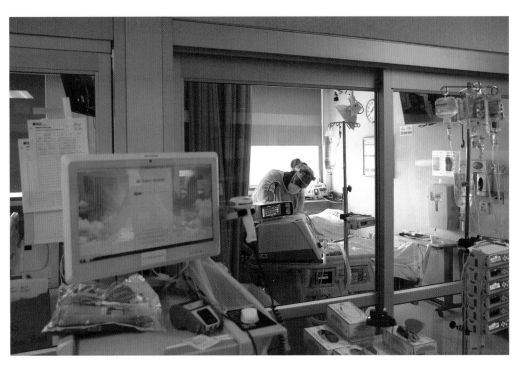

Figure 7.1 /   A medical worker inside a patient's room in a Covid-19 intensive care unit at Temple University Hospital in Philadelphia, April 7, 2020.

Photo by Tim Tai/*Philadelphia Inquirer*

LW / In terms of photos with people suffering from Covid, are you concerned with whether the portrayal shows them in a dignified manner?

DK / What we always try to do with any photograph is to document what happens and portray it accurately. I don't even know if it's a question of dignity when you're sick. If you've ever been really, really sick, it is incredibly difficult to focus on anything around you, even focus on the nurse who is trying to treat you, because you feel so terrible. That is the reality.

The truth is not always pretty, and I think there's a danger in editing those "ugly" kinds of photos out because you don't really show how horrible something can be.

When we discuss which images to publish, I'll ask the photographer: What happened before this photo? What happened after? Did you have the subject's permission? Was the subject lucid? Those *are* considerations I think about.

In the newsroom, we are inundated with graphic images, and photos of chaos and calamity all day long. My perspective of the world is so different from, say, my cousin's. When her kids go off to college, I'm saying, "Baby, be careful." She says, "Have a great time!" It's a different perspective because I almost know too much. I *am* the filter; I see what most other people don't. But you have to find a way to convey the gravity. There is a real risk when you don't document how horrific a situation, like Covid, is. When the public doesn't see it, they don't understand it or believe it.

LW / How do you determine what is too much, what won't be shown to the public?

DK / If I don't have enough information about a photo, then I will not run it. If I can't get background on an image—all the context of what was happening at that moment—then we can't publish it.

Truth is, early on, we weren't showing the really hard Covid photos because we just didn't have information. The country shut down in March and we didn't understand what was happening. What *is* this disease? What does it look like? What does it do? How do you get it? We didn't know how close, or not, you could get to people, which greatly impacts photojournalism because this field thrives on intimacy with the subject. And all of a sudden we're telling all our photographers, "Don't go into people's homes. Stay back." We weren't capturing the ravages of the disease. So instead we were showing the effects of the shutdown on the city, on businesses. Everything was closed. We have a lot of photos of people at their windows. Normally, the streets of Philadelphia are packed, but we showed the city as a ghost town. [See figure 7.2]

LW / Now, coming up toward a year after the shutdown, is the public fatigued by this coverage? If so, does that influence your photographers' work?

DK / The public is definitely experiencing Covid fatigue. I think it hit around September or October. But that doesn't change how our photographers operate. They are charged with documenting what is out there and not with varying their imagery or their coverage to suit the mood of the public. So it makes no difference to us, in terms of coverage, that the public is fatigued. Where it

Figure 7.2 / Local businesses are closed due to the coronavirus outbreak in Philadelphia, Pennsylvania, March 28, 2020.

Photo by Tyger Williams/*Philadelphia Inquirer*

does make a difference is that we see people relaxing their behaviors when it comes to the safety precautions, and that can put the photographers at risk. At a certain point early on, most people had masks, many had gloves. You just don't see as many people taking those steps these days.

LW / You must have also dealt with safety issues when your photographers covered protests.

DK / Philadelphia was one of the last big cities to explode after the death of George Floyd. I remember seeing the video of Floyd's death and thinking, this is not going to end well; there will be a reaction. Sure enough, so many cities started witnessing protests. One after the other, boom, boom, boom. And still, it hadn't hit us.

But then on Saturday [May 30], it started here. I went in that day, pulled out the bulletproof vests and helmets, and sent my staff a note, telling them I wasn't sure how the day would play out, but the equipment was ready for them. And sure enough, the city burned for several days and nights. During that time, we had almost all our staff documenting Philadelphia.[6]

I was rotating people to make sure they could get enough rest, because the work was nonstop. And it was dangerous. We had photographers robbed and beat up, and one had chemical burns.

We had taken so much care to keep photographers out of any dangerous Covid situations, canceling assignments if anything seemed uncertain, thinking through every detail. All of that went out the window with the protests. The George Floyd unrest erupted and now the staff was in crowds in order to work. It was the difference of being completely isolated and then thrown right into the chaos. It's not that we didn't think about Covid, but there were so many other things happening at once. At a certain point, I spoke with my deputy [the second highest-ranking editor in the Video and Photography department] and said, "We have exposed them all to Covid." I was adamant about the staff getting rest. I didn't want people run-down and their immune systems compromised by that. It was an absolutely dizzying three days, and when it finally settled down, the feeling was: where do we go from here?

LW / The photojournalists were handling so much at once. Did they have training—for instance, hostile environment training—to help them navigate this?[7]

DK / I do remember worrying that our people are not prepared for this if it gets violent. I have some veteran photographers and they had no problem; they are seasoned. But I also have very young photographers. They are fresh in this business. This was new for them. We did not have any across-the-board training in place for situations like this.

So after those three chaotic days, I called up some photographers who have conflict experience and asked them to do a training session with my staff. We did it via Zoom. Right after that, we hired someone who specializes in this for photographers, and she led a HEAT [hostile environment awareness training] session with us, again on Zoom. I had never imagined we would all require this. Sure, protests can be rowdy, maybe a car or two burning, but I hadn't anticipated anything like what actually happened here.

Figure 7.3 / Smoke rises from a burning police cruiser during the Justice for George Floyd Philadelphia protest, May 30, 2020.

Photo by Yong Kim/*Philadelphia Inquirer*

Figure 7.4 / Police readying to approach protesters at the George Floyd protest, Philadelphia, Pennsylvania, May 30, 2020.

Photo by Yong Kim/*Philadelphia Inquirer*

LW /   You mentioned robbery and assault. What happened? Who attacked the photographers?

DK / I hesitate to call the attackers "protesters," though they were among the people who were part of the demonstrating crowds. I had one photojournalist call me, "My arms are on fire. I'm burning!" My response was "Get out of there." He had burns from some chemical irritant.

I had another photographer call and say, "Someone just took my cameras." He continued working on his cell phone, but it didn't feel safe to me, so again my response was "Get out of there." I found out the next day that he had been smashed over the head, and then they took one of his [camera] bodies and broke the other.[8]

This is all in the same day, so it's kind of a blur. I had another photographer on site. She was good for a while; we were on the phone, going back and forth, doing check-ins. Then she called and said, "They just took my cameras and my laptop." She was trying to chase them down. My reaction again was about safety and I told her to leave.

So on top of all the Covid stress, we had this moment where the physical risks and harms were so intense. We didn't know whom to trust. Your photographers are out there trying to work and they're getting targeted. It was an especially exhausting moment for us.

As for who was committing these attacks, it's hard for me to say. The majority of people that were out there protesting had good intent, wanted their voices heard, and wanted to be seen standing against racial injustice. But some people will say, "That person took my picture. Whatever I have done has been documented" and they'll get angry about that.

LW / Did this ever lead to conversations, inside the newsroom, about whether you would intentionally obscure identities of protesters, or of demonstrators committing acts like vandalism or theft?

DK / Well, we don't publish photos where a face is blurred. That's not how to handle this. We document events as they are. And, in fact, we did run a lot of photos of vandalism, looting, and similar acts. But that can create risk for the journalist. So in terms of photographer safety, one option we offered was to withhold bylines from photos. Particular pictures were published without the photographer's name credited to the image.[9]

We had people going after our journalists on Twitter. We were worried about doxxing.[10] We had a photographer who was approached by a protester who recognized her because other protesters had posted video of her.

LW / Did things ease up after the late May and early June protests?

DK / It never really stopped—not the protests, but the pace at which we had to work that year. First Covid, then George Floyd, and then of course the presidential election. About a week before that, I told my staff, "Everyone needs to rest. It'll be an intense pace as of election day." But that rest never came because we had the killing of Walter Wallace Jr., a young Black man with a mental condition who was shot by police in Philadelphia.[11] That was October and we again saw chaos and unrest in the city.[12] And then the election on the heels of that, and of course Philadelphia is huge in that story. We had protests, Trump supporters versus anti-Trump, outside the Convention Center [where hundreds of thousands of mail-in ballots were counted].[13]

Figure 7.5 / Police officers with shields line up in West Philadelphia during protests and civil unrest sparked by the fatal police shooting of Walter Wallace Jr., October 26, 2020.

Photo by Jessica Griffin/*Philadelphia Inquirer*

This has been a physically grueling year for the newsroom. It has also been a very traumatizing year. One thing that newspapers and newsrooms do not do well is to go back and sort things out. I'm telling my staff, "If you need to talk to somebody, a therapist, please do." But meanwhile, I'm going on with the program because I have to work. And so you don't really think about it. You move on to the next thing and we don't have routine ways of decompressing—especially now when you can't even hang out with friends or take a trip to the beach, because of Covid. We went through a lot that year and I think anyone who worked as a journalist in 2020 is going to need to spend some time really processing how dramatic and traumatic this was.

LW / You've said that the job of the photojournalist is to document what is happening. Of course photojournalists, like everyone else, hold opinions, and sometimes about the issues they cover. Should the public know of these opinions and subjectivities? Would the public be better served if they knew more about who the individual person behind the lens is?

DK / If we are talking about allowing subjectivities or biases into the work, then we are no longer talking about journalism. As for captions, they should be neutral, giving the details of what happened, of what we see in the image. There should be no commentary.

In terms of the visuals, we need to cover all sides of any situation. No matter, say, who you voted for or what you believe, you need to be able to cover fairly. You can't be an activist in your work. I just want you to be able to tell the truth with your camera.

It was a difficult year for many and especially a very difficult year to be a Black journalist. It can be incredibly hard to focus after you have watched a video of a Black man, who could be your father or brother, pinned down by another man's knee while he passes away.[14] You see the life leave his body. I can't separate that from who I am. I can't say, "I'm not a Black woman" because I am. And that video affected me enormously. But I also have to be able to look at photos of every situation, including those in response to situations of police brutality, and ask: Is this true? Does this portray truth?

In this sense, I think it can be dangerous for a journalist to publicly also be an activist or to present their opinions openly, on social media or elsewhere. It blurs the lines. Then people will ask: So what is it you're *really* saying [with this photo]? What is your agenda?

As journalists, we put the information out there for people to make a decision. I'm not going to tell you what decision to make. We'll put the facts out there so people are able to ask questions, able to form their opinions on whether, for instance, they should criticize misuses of authority. But I'm not going to tell you, *this* is what you should think.

LW / Should publications work to cultivate, support, and encourage photographers of color?

DK / Definitely. The pipeline is so important. In terms of photo editing alone, to my knowledge, there are maybe four Black women, including myself, who are DoPs [Directors of Photography] in some form of a traditional newsroom in the entire country. We have to do a much better job in cultivating this for a wider group.

Newsrooms need to be diverse, and not just in terms of race. I think age diversity is very important. For instance, veteran photographers can be teachers for a younger generation. Diversity is vital for the exchange of knowledge and skills across individuals, and so that you have a plurality of approaches, of different personalities and styles in your newsroom. I have some photographers who will walk into fire and others who are more reserved and see in quieter ways.

In terms of story generation, knowledge exchange, and approach, it's critical that you have a healthy balance, whether we mean age or gender or sexual orientation or race, because you're also talking about how your newsroom reflects the communities you cover. I have a woman on my staff now who is pregnant, and she brings insights from that perspective to the table. If we're all bringing a different dish to the table, you are not only eating a large meal, but will have different, fantastic flavors. But if we're all bringing, you know, an apple to the table, then yeah, you'll be full, but it just won't be fulfilling.

LW / Should the pregnant woman be assigned to cover the maternal story, or the LBGTQ+ photographer to the gay rights story, or the Black photographer to Black Lives Matter stories? Or does that not inform how you give assignments?

DK / If a Black photographer pitches a story that happens to be in a Black neighborhood, and that's something they want to photograph, then go for it. If I'm assigning, I'm not just keeping identity in mind; I'm also thinking about people's schedules, who is available to cover a story when we need it photographed. And certainly identity doesn't always play a role, but sometimes it does. For example, we're working on a prostitution story about a young woman, and so we needed women to photograph that story. But that isn't the only way these decisions are made and we definitely don't have a "Black beat" for Black photographers and no "LBGTQ beat" for LBGTQ photographers, and so forth.

LW / Reflecting back on 2020 and then looking ahead, what observations or insights can you offer?

DK / 2020 was an incredible year for photojournalism and photojournalists. Some of the coverage was historic. But it was also incredible in very hard ways. We lost so much intimacy. The 16–35mm or the 24–70mm, that's the photographer's bliss, those shorter-range lenses. And so much of last year had to be documented at arm's length.

Another heavy facet of 2020 was the way that journalists were targeted. We lost the safety of documenting, of doing the work without having that weight on us. Our sole mission is to bring the facts so that everybody can be informed and can make decisions. But there was a new public hatred of photographers and journalists that we saw in 2020, and unfortunately, I just don't know if that will ever roll back, if it will ever be the way it was before.

NOTES

1   This interview with Kenon was conducted in early 2021. The *Philadelphia Inquirer*, founded in 1829, is the third-oldest continuously operating daily newspaper in the US. Serving largely the greater Philadelphia metropolitan area, the paper has a significant weekday circulation, and it has earned twenty Pulitzer Prizes.

2   Griffin is an award-wining photographer on staff at the *Philadelphia Inquirer*. For the piece Kenon describes, see Wendy Ruderman (reporter) and Jessica Griffin (photographer), "Medics on the front line," *Philadelphia Inquirer*, April 30, 2020, https://www.inquirer.com/health/coronavirus/a/coronavirus-covid19-main-line-narberth-paramedics-20200430.html.

3   Kenon refers to the CDC's then-recommended fourteen-day quarantine period after potential exposure to Covid-19.

4   HIPAA rules bar media from spaces where patients' protected information, for instance about their health and identity, is accessible, if media does not have the patient's prior authorization. With hospital permission, media may be allowed in such spaces, but still are required to document in a way that protects patient privacy.

5 For the piece Kenon references, see Wendy Ruderman (reporter) and Jessica Griffin (photographer), "A Dose of Hope," *Philadelphia Inquirer*, February 10, 2021, https://www.inquirer.com/health/coronavirus/a/coronavirus-health-care-workers-inside-philadelphia-hospitals-20210210.html. The article includes images where patients, some of whom are identified by name and are visually identifiable, share personal details, such as one 69-year-old woman who describes how Covid took the lives of twenty-five of her relatives and friends, and how she had not been able to hug her children or grandchildren for nearly a year.

6 During these days, Philadelphia witnessed peaceful protests but also more volatile acts, including the burning of police cars and at least one building. The Pennsylvania National Guard was called in, and SWAT officers used tear gas and pepper spray on protesters. The city had nightly curfews.

7 Hostile environment training workshops teach safety and survival measures to professionals (often journalists) in order to prepare them for dangerous or volatile settings and to raise awareness around broader security measures.

8 The camera body is the main part of a digital camera and includes the image sensor and digital circuitry. It is distinguished from the camera lens.

9 See, for instance, Inquirer Staff Photographers, "Philadelphia Photos: Center City vandalized, looted following protests over George Floyd killing," *Philadelphia Inquirer*, May 30, 2020, https://www.inquirer.com/photo/philadelphians-gather-mourn-george-floyd-20200530.html#loaded. Certain images are credited merely as "staff."

10 Doxxing is the digital dissemination of private or identifying information (such as one's home address), often with malicious intent.

11 Walter Wallace Jr. was shot by police on October 26, 2020, in Philadelphia, Pennsylvania. Wallace was having a mental health crisis. The killing was caught on a bystander's cell phone and the video was posted to social media.

12 Philadelphia witnessed protests through the end of October in the wake of Wallace's killing. The mostly peaceful protests also involved acts of looting and altercations with police.

13 With its twenty electoral votes, Pennsylvania plays a pivotal role in any US presidential election. In 2020, over 350,000 mail-in ballots were counted at the Philadelphia Convention Center. This led to political protests, with demonstrators demanding that the "Count the Vote" move forward, and opposition voices, primarily in support of President Trump, questioning the legitimacy of the ballot tally.

14 Kenon refers to the cell phone video that documents the killing of George Floyd. In June 2021, Darnella Frazier, who recorded the video, won a special citation from the Pulitzer Prize committee.

8 MARYANNE GOLON

MARYANNE GOLON *is the Director of Photography at the* Washington Post. *Since she joined the* Post, *the newspaper has won a Pulitzer Prize for photography. Prior to this position, she was Director of Photography for* Time magazine. *During her tenure at* Time *she oversaw the photography teams that produced the magazine's special Hurricane Katrina edition as well as its unique black-bordered 9/11 edition. Both won National Magazine Awards for single topics. Golon has also won numerous picture editing awards from the National Press Photographers Association and the Pictures of the Year International competition.*

Golon has been the Jury Chair for World Press Photo, faculty for the Joop Swart Masterclass and the Missouri Photo Workshop, the Chairperson for the Eddie Adams Workshop Board of Directors, and Chair of the professional advisory board for NOOR photo agency, among other titles.

LAUREN WALSH / What were the *Washington Post*'s safety protocols for photo coverage of Covid-19? And how do you balance between the journalist's safety and the public's need to see and know?[1]

MARYANNE GOLON / The number one position of the management of the *Washington Post* is that no one should go into any situation in which they do not feel comfortable. Anybody with underlying conditions, anybody who's taking care of a sick or immune-compromised person, anyone at all—the expectation was that you did not have to do any assignment if you didn't want to. Number two, we provide PPE, meaning that we have KN95 masks and gloves and the wipes to clean equipment, and hand sanitizer to clean your hands after you've taken off gloves. For those who took on these assignments, the idea was to work in as safe as possible a manner.

Staff photographer Michael Williamson, for example, was adamant.[2] He wanted to cover this, wanted to get inside a hospital to document up close, firsthand, the ravages of the disease. At that point, we spoke to the hospital where he would work. We had to ensure safety. We had to know, for instance, he would have assistance donning and doffing the PPE after being in a coronavirus ward, because medical professionals are expert at this, but photojournalists aren't, and taking one class about how to put on and take off PPE is not sufficient in these highly viral environments where people are dying.

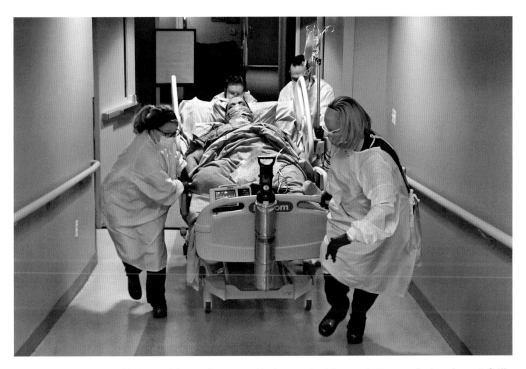

Figure 8.1 /   Marya Chaisson, left, a pulmonary critical care physician, and other medical workers at Griffin Hospital in Derby, Connecticut, race to move patient Jose Vasquez, twenty-eight, from a Covid-19 wing to the intensive care unit after his condition worsens, May 5, 2020.

Photo by Michael S. Williamson/*Washington Post*

And then after this work, Michael would quarantine immediately for two weeks in case there was any issue. In terms of a human cost, it's not a question: you do what you need to keep people safe. But the business cost is that you take somebody off the roster for two weeks.

As editor, I personally was very concerned about photographers' gear. This was especially so in the very beginning of the pandemic when we were all quarantining our grocery bags in the hallway because we were afraid to touch anything. It was terrifying. So I needed to know that the photographers who were covering higher-risk Covid stories were protected. But how do you clean the camera equipment? The questions were always: How long does the virus last on surfaces? Will we be safe?

LW / Many have said that despite a higher death toll, the visual coverage of Covid-19, particularly in the United States, has been less explicitly graphic than the coverage we saw, for instance, of another disease outbreak—the Ebola outbreak, in parts of Africa, in 2014 and 2015.[3] Is that true, in your opinion?

MG / These images [Figures 8.2 and 8.3] ran in the *Post* on April 22.[4] That was still the early days of the pandemic. The story was about avoiding the loneliness of a coronavirus hospital death. This was in Italy, which was hit extremely hard early in the pandemic.

The photographer is Gianluca Panella.[5] He's a freelance photojournalist, and he spent a long time working on this. He ended up doing a whole story on this man, a former Navy sailor, named Carmelo, whose family decided not to take him to the hospital even when he was very sick.

This picture [Figure 8.2] was quite controversial when we published it. That's Carmelo's grandson in the striped shirt and the others, in PPE, are ambulance crew. They came to administer CPR, but Carmelo was dead. And then, you see his family in the doorway, responding to his death [Figure 8.3]. They didn't want him to go to the hospital because they knew that if he went, he wouldn't be with family.

This family was absolutely adamant that these pictures be shown. They felt that people need to see what this disease does. They love Carmelo and they didn't see this as disrespectful to him. They viewed it as informing the public of the ravages of the disease.

We had pictures from Ebola coverage that were also controversial, and again, it was important to bring that situation to public attention.[6] We work to show the truth to the best of our ability.

Sometimes, if you're in a private setting, you're following certain rules; for instance, in a hospital, you're following their protocols in terms of what you can and cannot photograph. Here's one image [Figure 8.4] from inside a medical facility in California. The photographer, Melina Mara, wasn't allowed in the room you see in the image.[7] But she nevertheless creates a beautiful composition within such restrictions.

Getting back to the larger question, the truth is, we produce so much content. I'm constantly amazed by what people see as much as I am by what they *don't* see, because we do have an

Figure 8.2 / Carmelo Marchese, ninety-three, a former sailor with the Italian Navy, is lifted by emergency responders and his grandson Stefano (striped shirt). The responders administered CPR, but were unable to revive Carmelo.

© Gianluca Panella

Figure 8.3 / Carmelo's granddaughter Elisa arrives to join her grieving mother and brother.

© Gianluca Panella

Figure 8.4 / Nurses and respiratory specialists treat coronavirus patients, with a doctor phoning in, at El Centro Regional Medical Center in El Centro, California, May 24, 2020.

Photo by Melina Mara/*Washington Post*

incredible breadth of coverage. So some people might feel there is no explicit coverage, but there is, and it is important work.

LW / As Director of Photography, you were overseeing multiple major stories this year, not only the pandemic but also the Black Lives Matter protests that shook the US. Can photography be a tool to correct racial injustices that exist in American society?

MG / Photography can always be used as a tool. But it depends on who's wielding the tool— that matters. One of the conversations that's been percolating all around the photo community is the legacy, in the US and in Europe—and I'm consciously adding Europe—of the white male gaze, which has brought us the world in pictures for such a long time.[8] That means, for instance, that you had to be rich enough to be able to afford the equipment. That's just one factor of many that made it possible for wealthy white males to be the purveyors of journalistic photography in places all around the world.

This is significant because it informs the photography we see. There is a white male gaze. As there is a female gaze, and a person of color gaze, and so forth. What I mean is that obviously the person behind the camera is deciding what to show you and what to photograph and how to photograph it.

So the critical question is: is what the photographer sees truly representative of what's out there? And ever more, the next question is: are the people who are chosen by the photo editor to take the pictures members of the community that is being documented, or are they parachuting in?

Getting back to racial injustice, in order to change the current situation, there needs to be more understanding of the underlying issues. I don't know if photography can be a tool to *correct* racial injustices in this country, but it can be a tool to expose them. It can be a tool to explain.

And no matter who's holding the camera, the underlying ethics of photojournalism should be the same. Every photographer should approach everything that they cover with an open mind and an empathetic perspective.

LW / If the underlying ethics are always the same, then regarding coverage of race in the United States today, does the ethnic or racial identity of the photographer on that story matter?

MG / Well, our primary photographers covering race-related matters for the *Washington Post* in 2020 have mostly been people of color, not just African American, but people of color.

With the Black Lives Matter movement, we've seen a reawakening on race, a reckoning. It's a wake-up call—broadly but also inside the industry—to seeing other points of view.

LW / How does this play out in practice?

MG / It's not so much about what the photographer literally sees; it's that they may be drawn to stories because they recognize them as important stories that need to be told.

For instance, we have a multipart series called "George Floyd's America."[9] The first installment, as an example, provides a deep background on Floyd. What was his life like? Where is he from? What shaped him?

This whole project started with photographer Joshua Lott, because he was in Houston [Texas] for George Floyd's funeral and burial.[10] He went to the neighborhood where Floyd had grown up and started talking to people. And one of the individuals, who inspired the series and becomes a main character in it, was a person that Joshua found just by talking to people, with his camera at his side, not in front of his face. Joshua was drawn in this direction.

Stepping back from the specifics of that series, having a diversity of perspectives doesn't refer to something qualitative about the photographs themselves. It's not a difference in photographic training. It's not about better or worse photographs. It's about being pulled to diverse parts of a story because maybe the photographer has experience with *this* topic, or because *that* aspect is personally meaningful. And then that resonance opens a door that maybe another photographer would have left closed.

Figure 8.5 / A new mural honoring "Big Floyd" covers the back wall of Scott Food Mart near Cuney Homes, the oldest public housing project in Houston, Texas, June 9, 2020. Other community members who have died, mostly from street violence, are also memorialized on the corner store's walls.

Photo by Joshua Lott/*Washington Post*

LW / Was that project, "George Floyd's America," an attempt to visualize institutional racism in the US?

MG / Yes, it was. We're trying to tell the much bigger, longer story behind Floyd's death. So we're tackling how systemic racism shaped Floyd's life and hobbled his ambitions. We are looking at housing, at health care, at policing, at prisons. We're asking: how did we get to where we are right now in this moment in the history of the United States? It is an exploration of, as the piece is titled, George Floyd's America.

The series has a multiplicity of reporters and photographers—again, that idea of diversity. When you have varied journalists who are smart, sensitive, practiced, diverse in style and experience, then you get great work.[11]

LW / Is there enough of this diversity in American newsrooms right now?

MG / There is *not* enough diversity. This is fact-based. Look at the statistics.[12] I think newsrooms are like all of corporate America; they're largely run by white males.

So the newsrooms don't represent the breadth of society. You go no place but up by having more and more journalists covering communities where the people in those communities feel comfortable speaking with somebody who looks like them, who talks like them, who comes from their background. Diversity is critical. I think at times you even have a better chance of a deeper understanding of what's happening in certain communities. You can build stronger trust with those communities in order to tell their important stories.

Journalism is about a curiosity in the world. There is a very first-person element to that. That drives individual journalists to seek out what matters. So the more diversity you have across the storytelling, the better the journalism will be. One would hope.

LW /   In terms of covering the major 2020 protests, did any *Washington Post* photographers face threats or harassment?

MG / We had photographers who were arrested while on assignment, for instance, in Minneapolis. In one case, our photographer Joshua Lott was kettled, swept up along with other journalists and protesters.[13] He told the officers at least six times that he was a journalist with the *Washington Post*. Finally, someone listened and called a higher ranking officer who said that as a journalist he must be released. But meanwhile, Joshua had been confined and his hands had been bound with heavy-duty zip ties.

The situation wound up defused. But still, Joshua had a sore hand, and that shouldn't have happened. He was covering as a journalist, not there as a protester. [See Figure 8.6]

Joshua was harassed another time, too. Also by police, but in Kenosha [Wisconsin]. He was in a car, caravanning with a group of journalists. They were moving from one protest site to another.[14] The sites were blocks apart and the police were trailing him. Maybe it's a coincidence that Joshua is African American and this happens specifically to *him*, but I doubt it. Eventually,

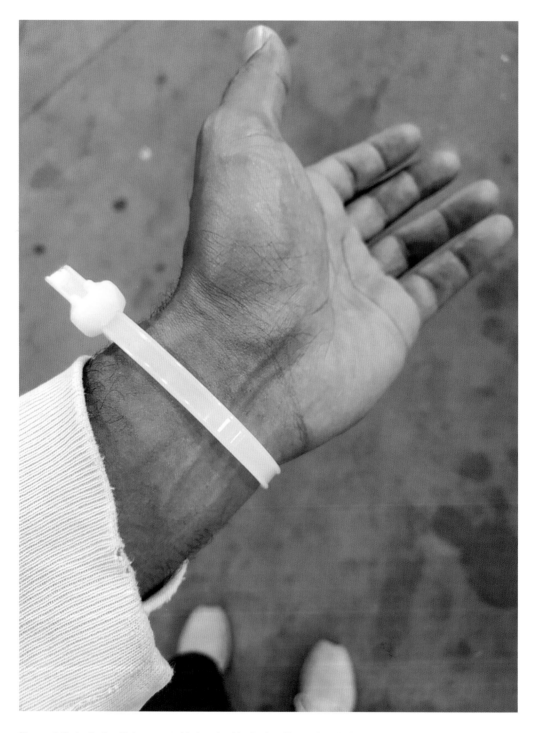

Figure 8.6 / Lott self-documents his hand, with zip tie still on, after the binding around both hands has been cut, Minneapolis, Minnesota, May 31, 2020.

© Joshua Lott

he was pulled over. A journalist colleague in the car behind also stopped to make sure Joshua would be alright. The officer told Joshua he was "driving in circles" and that's why he pulled him over. Meanwhile, another officer stepped out of the cruiser and approached the second vehicle [driven by Lott's colleague, a journalist with Getty Images], and stood there with his long gun prominently out. That's terrifying.

In the end, the officers couldn't charge Joshua with anything and as it happened, just then protesters turned down that street. It doesn't look good to have two white cops pulling over a Black man, so the officers left. Again, the situation was diffused. But you know, these circumstances are upsetting.

Obviously, it is very stressful for the photojournalist to be involved in that, and it's nerve-wracking for me as editor to hear that an officer had his gun out. I care about the people who are working for us. To put the risks in perspective: we require that all our photographers who cover protests have health insurance and professional insurance. Professional insurance protects their equipment if something happens to it. This isn't to treat human matters with dollar signs, but to explain that the risks are very real and our journalists face them in order to get the news.

LW /   Will the bodies of photographic work, on Covid and Black Lives Matter, remain significant into the future?

MG / Of course they will. News is the first rough draft of history. You're running and gunning at a breakneck pace to bring the news on a minute-by-minute basis. But later, you can get out of the weeds and up in the canopy for a different historical perspective. All of this coverage helps with that.

What we do is tell the story with photographs, and we tell from the perspective of being in the moment. Journalism comes from a pure place. You are trying very hard to say, "Here is what happened right now."

We were there; we were witnesses. That's the draft of history. And then the historians will figure out a greater context over a much longer period of time.

NOTES

1   This interview with Golon was conducted in fall 2020. The *Washington Post*, founded in 1877, is an American daily newspaper, with a large national circulation, that has won over sixty Pulitzer Prizes.

2   Williamson, a staff photographer with the *Washington Post* since 1993, has won two Pulitzer Prizes.

3   The West African Ebola virus epidemic began in Guinea in late 2013. It is sometimes referred to as the 2014 Ebola outbreak. Death tolls for this severe outbreak were highest in Guinea, Sierra Leone, and Liberia. Globally, over 10,000 people died. In March 2016, the World Health Organization concluded the "Public

Health Emergency of International Concern" status of the outbreak. For more on the debate about a potential disparity in terms of graphic coverage of Ebola versus Covid, see, for example, Patrick Gathara, "Should images of coronavirus victims be sanitised?" Al Jazeera, June 7, 2020, https://www.aljazeera.com/opinions/2020/6/7/should-images-of-coronavirus-victims-be-sanitised.

4   See the article: Chico Harlan, Stefano Pitrelli, and Gianluca Panella, "Avoiding the loneliness of a coronavirus hospital death," *Washington Post*, April 22, 2020, https://www.washingtonpost.com/world/2020/04/22/avoiding-loneliness-coronavirus-hospital-death/.

5   Panella is an award-winning Italian freelance photojournalist who has covered social issues, conflict, and political upheaval around the globe.

6   For some of the *Washington Post*'s explicit coverage of the Ebola outbreak of 2014–15, see, for instance, Lena H. Sun, "Global response to Ebola marked by lack of coordination and leadership, experts say," *Washington Post*, September 11, 2014, https://www.washingtonpost.com/national/health-science/global-response-to-ebola-marked-by-lack-of-coordination-and-leadership-experts-say/2014/09/11/35365264-39dc-11e4-8601-97ba88884ffd_story.html.

7   Mara, an award-winning photojournalist, has been on staff with the *Post* since 2004. For the full article and images from the medical facility Mara documented, see Kevin Sieff (reporter) and Melina Mara (photographer), "Coronavirus on the border," *Washington Post*, May 27, 2020, https://www.washingtonpost.com/world/2020/05/27/coronavirus-mexico-border/.

8   The "male gaze," a concept first introduced in the early 1970s, became a subject of discussion within feminist studies to critique media representations of women. The white male gaze adds a component of ethnicity/nationality to this critique. For more on this, see, for instance, Savannah Dodd and Andrew Jackson, "'Good' photographs: The white male gaze and how we privilege ways of seeing," Witness (website), May 10, 2019, https://witness.worldpressphoto.org/good-photographs-the-white-male-gaze-and-how-we-privilege-ways-of-seeing-30ac3f005acc.

9   See the series: (*Washington Post* Staff) Arelis R. Hernández, Tracy Jan, Laura Meckler, Toluse Olorunnipa, Robert Samuels, Griff Witte, and Cleve R. Wootson, Jr. (writing) and Salwan Georges, Tamir Kalifa, Joshua Lott, Montinique Monroe, and Michael Starghill, Jr. (photography), "George Floyd's America," *Washington Post*, October 26, 2020, https://www.washingtonpost.com/nation/2020/10/12/george-floyd-america/.

10 Lott, who was a sought-after freelance photojournalist for more than fifteen years, joined the *Washington Post* as a staff photographer in 2020. His work has been featured in publications around the world.

11 Golon adds, "The *Washington Post* has been at the forefront of this for several years. We won a Pulitzer Prize for national reporting for the database that shows how many people, of what race, have been killed by police. It reflects the patterns of racial injustice that exist in this country." See the database: Julie Tate, Jennifer Jenkins, and Steven Rich, "Fatal Force," *Washington Post*, 2015–ongoing, https://www.washingtonpost.com/graphics/investigations/police-shootings-database/.

12 For statistics, see, for instance, Elizabeth Grieco, "Newsroom employees are less diverse than US workers overall," Fact Tank / Pew Research Center (website), November 2, 2018, https://www.pewresearch.org/fact-tank/2018/11/02/newsroom-employees-are-less-diverse-than-u-s-workers-overall/, or Jesse Holcomb and Helen Stubbs, "In US, views of diversity in news vary by party ID, race," Knight Foundation, June 25, 2020, https://knightfoundation.org/articles/in-u-s-views-of-diversity-in-news-vary-by-party-id-race/. See also the Introduction of *Through the Lens*.

13 Kettling is a method of crowd control, where a cordon of police officers surrounds and confines a crowd to a small area. Crowd members are either forced to exit through a controlled outlet, or they are prevented from exiting and are arrested.

14 Jacob Blake, a Black man, was shot seven times in the back by police in Kenosha, Wisconsin, on August 23, 2020. The city was the site of days of protests and unrest in the wake of this killing.

AFTERWORD

2020 was a historically tumultuous year, and it is my hope for the world that the subsequent years are somehow not so fraught with crisis.

Through the Lens: The Pandemic and Black Lives Matter is not intended to be a fully comprehensive take on all issues that photojournalism grappled with in 2020. I believe strongly in listening to and learning from thoughtful representative voices, those who have experiences on the ground. And I have faith that such voices can inspire ever greater curiosity and, importantly, critical thinking in the reading audience, deepening the understanding of news photography and the role it plays in shaping our world.

The future will present new challenges, new ethical conundrums, and new controversies in the realm of photojournalism. *Through the Lens* has aimed to provide a greater sensitivity to such issues—those that have occurred already and those yet to come. Ultimately, I hope to instill an appreciation for visual journalism itself. It is a form of news that can move the world when done well, and it is a genre that can positively change things when done responsibly.

—LW

ACKNOWLEDGMENTS

As with any large effort, it takes a village. I am grateful to all who helped with reading of drafts, making introductions, brainstorming, giving or facilitating use of imagery, and generally being highly supportive of me and my work. The list of wonderful people includes: Evan Benn, Richard Chen, Sandy Ciric, Pamela Cruz, Colin Dickey, Ashley Gilbertson, Elizabeth Krist, Olivier Laurent, Christopher Lee, Joshua Lott, Matthew Lutts, Keith Miller, Santiago Lyon, Caitlin Ochs, Gianluca Panella, Laura Roumanos, Javier Ruiz, Maggie Steber, Sara Terry, Jen Vennall, Stacy Walsh, Vivian Xing, and Stephenie Young. Ron Haviv was especially instrumental with his support through this process. And an extra special thanks to Alex Ginsberg for his help throughout, and to Isabelle and Annaliese.

I thank NYU's Gallatin School of Individualized Study for granting financial support for this project, and especially my gratitude to Dean Susanne L. Wofford, who has always provided unwavering belief in my work.

The photo organizations that have helped make this book with photographs possible include: the Associated Press, Getty Images, NOOR, the *Philadelphia Inquirer*, Redux, Reuters, VII, and the *Washington Post*. My thanks to them all.

My deepest thanks to Spencer Green for his incredible dedication and his excellence in fact checking; to Joanna Scutts for her brilliance in editing and for her insistence that we share a cocktail; to Stephanie Leone, once my student and now a friend and colleague, for making this book look so well designed; and to Carrie Messina and Carly Harrison for offering expert eyes to proofread the book in its final stages.

Natalie Foster, of Routledge, has gone above and beyond in supporting me and bringing this forward. I couldn't have asked for a better editor. I am indebted. Likewise, Mary Bisbee-Beek has been crucial to the conception, growth, and fruition of this work, and I am profoundly grateful for the encouragement, the dedication, and the friendship.

Finally, my heartfelt appreciation for all the interviewees who gave their time, passion, and commitment to this work. I am honored to learn from their experiences and humbled by their dedication to journalistic practice.

INDEX